KRISHNA

THE
MANAGEMENT
GURU

Sunita Pant Bansal started writing poems and stories at the age of eight and has not stopped since. Trained in Nutrition, she practiced as a nutritionist for a couple of years before deciding to follow her passion instead. In her four decades of writing career, she founded a weekend newspaper and three magazines, besides editing five magazines, writing numerous articles and producing a short film.

Sunita hails from the Kumaon hills of the Himalayas, a region well-known for its crop of litterateurs. With that pedigree, it was no wonder that she started exploring mythology and its impact on our culture. In her writing career of 40 years, Sunita has authored hundreds of books for children and young adults on folk literature and mythology. For adults, her genres cover body, mind and soul, her books being sold in multiple languages globally. Her forte is decoding Hindu scriptures to show their relevance and application in today's times. Sunita's bestsellers include *Kailas Mansarovar: The Journey of Body, Mind and Soul*, *Ramayan: The Journey of Ram,* and *Mahabharat: The Rise and Fall of Heroes.*

KRISHNA

THE MANAGEMENT GURU

SUNITA PANT BANSAL

RUPA

Published by
Rupa Publications India Pvt. Ltd 2020
7/16, Ansari Road, Daryaganj
New Delhi 110002

Sales centres:
Bengaluru Chennai
Hyderabad Jaipur Kathmandu
Kolkata Mumbai Prayagraj

Copyright © Sunita Pant Bansal 2020

All rights reserved.
No part of this publication may be reproduced, transmitted,
or stored in a retrieval system, in any form or by any means,
electronic, mechanical, photocopying, recording or otherwise,
without the prior permission of the publisher.

The views and opinions expressed in this book are the author's
own and the facts are as reported by her which have been verified
to the extent possible, and the publishers are not in any way
liable for the same.

P-ISBN: 978-93-89967-95-1
E-ISBN: 978-93-90260-01-0

Third impression 2024

10 9 8 7 6 5 4 3

The moral right of the author has been asserted.

Printed in India

This book is sold subject to the condition that it shall not,
by way of trade or otherwise, be lent, resold, hired out, or otherwise
circulated, without the publisher's prior consent, in any form of
binding or cover other than that in which it is published.

Contents

Author's Note	*vii*
1. Krishna on Leadership	1
2. Krishna on Power	12
3. Krishna on Strategy	20
4. Krishna on Team Building	30
5. Krishna on Communication	41
6. Krishna on Work-Life Balance	49
7. Krishna on Rules	60
8. Krishna on Stability	69
9. Krishna on Behaviour	78
10. Krishna on Decision-Making	87
11. Krishna on Justifiable Means	99
12. Krishna on Non-Justifiable Means	108
13. Krishna on Goals	117
14. Krishna on Personal Growth	126
15. Krishna on Vision Statement	135
16. Krishna on Karma	144
17. Krishna on Work Etiquette	154
18. Krishna on Time Management	164
19. Krishna on Greed	175
20. Krishna on Loyalty	185
Acknowledgments	195

Author's Note

Krishna's global popularity can be gauged from the fact that Jack Sparrow, the protagonist of the series of five films, *Pirates of the Caribbean*, is based on Krishna. Ted Elliot, one of the screenwriters of the series, admits, 'While writing the character sketch of Jack Sparrow, we referred to the description of Lord Krishna, various shades of the Almighty, which helped us a lot in bringing the whole character of Jack Sparrow into existence.'

The keywords here are 'various shades'.

Krishna is a much-revered Hindu god, an incarnation of Lord Vishnu on earth. His one-point agenda for being born was to rid the world of the evil forces ruling it at that time, and unify the land under one righteous ruler. It was no mean task, and Krishna set about doing it as soon as he got a chance, right from his infancy.

The various shades of Krishna's character are visible all through his life. He was a loving and respectful son, a loyal and protective brother and friend, a passionate lover and spouse, a wise and dependable guide, a brilliant strategist and an invincible adversary.

Out of the vast palette of Krishna's shades, I have picked up those that define him as a 'management guru'. Guru means 'master', the best, the most superior, etc.—the list can go on.

I have culled out anecdotes from Krishna's life, including his stint in the great war of Mahabharata, which exemplify his traits as a strategist par excellence. Had he been present in this age, he would surely have been topping *Forbes*' list of 100 Most Influential or Powerful Men of the World.

Krishna started showing these traits very early in life, though they became more noticeable during his teenage. That was the time when people around him started taking him a bit more seriously. He developed a fan following of sorts, which continued to grow all through his life and after, and is still growing today.

In the initial phase of his life, Krishna was a cowherd and lived with other cowherds, although he belonged to the warrior class. As he grew up, his warring skills became evident, though he always favoured non-violence himself. He always tried to resolve the biggest of issues using peaceful means, by discussing and reasoning across the table, so to speak. He was capable of outwitting anyone in a discussion, and making them see the right path.

Krishna encouraged people to use their power of inference in deciding what 'dharma' or the right behaviour, was. He put greater stress on one's personal discretion and less on blindly following established beliefs. This is what makes him so endearing, so different from the other gods. Krishna did not sit on a pedestal and preach; he was a living example of what he taught. He actually walked the talk.

Krishna preached only once, and that too because he had to. Right in the middle of the battlefield of Kurukshetra, Arjun, the best Pandava warrior, panicked. Krishna, being his charioteer, his driver, had to steer him back to the right direction. As a good driver, that was his duty. The lecture Krishna gave to Arjun on the battlefield is called the Bhagavad Gita.

Even that philosophy of Krishna was utilitarian, contrary to what one would expect a 'lecture' to be. He denounced both the existing philosophies of that time: those of world-shunning spirituality and world-grasping materialism. Both were extremes. Krishna favoured moderation, the middle path.

Krishna's style of teaching was always informal, albeit with a dash of humour. He would essentially give tips—effective ones at that. Interestingly, the same are useful in managing an organization as well.

What we do at a macro level in our lives, the goals we set for ourselves, the roadmaps that we create to achieve them, the resources that we collect to help us on our journey, the savings we accrue for rainy days, the people we handle as we go along...all of these are done at a micro level in an organization. The guiding principles remain the same.

I have taken up 20 aspects of good leadership in this book: leadership, power, strategy, team building, communication, work-life balance, rules, stability, behaviour, decision making, justifiable means, non-justifiable means, goals, personal growth, vision statement, karma, work etiquette, time management, greed and loyalty. How Krishna dealt with them is reflected in his life.

I am presenting Krishna as an extraordinary individual, a smart guy, whom anyone would like to befriend. He is an ideal friend, philosopher and guide, one who can resolve our toughest of tensions over a cappuccino, or jog with us in the morning and set our self-doubts to rest, or take a leisurely stroll with us in the evening and change our perspective towards anything in life without us ever noticing the change.

And he would do all this and more without ever judging us.

Aren't these the desired qualities of an effective leader, a firebrand CEO?!

All through the book, I have quoted successful entrepreneurs, businessmen, presidents, emperors, statesmen, philosophers, educationists, motivational gurus and management professionals from all across the globe, echoing Krishna's thoughts. This is to show how globally relevant his philosophy was, and still is.

I have a learnt a lot from Krishna, and through this book I have tried to share that with my readers. If I manage to touch even one heart, change even one life, for the better, I would consider my goal accomplished.

1.

Krishna on Leadership

Leadership is not a title, it is a behaviour.

The simplest meaning of 'lead' is 'to guide'. Likewise, the simplest definition of leadership is the art of motivating a group of people to act towards a common goal.

As children, we always knew who the head of the family was, or the leader among the siblings. In school, too, being the class monitor was always a big thing. At that age, perhaps we did not realize the responsibility that went with the tag of 'head' or 'leader' or 'monitor'; we were more aware of the fact that these people were always blamed for any misdemeanour on the part of the others.

In an organization, a leader has a much tougher job than in a family or a classroom scenario. There are no relatives or friends to fall back on, nor does our age matter. The only thing that matters is our own skill-set for handling fellow humans. We could be the best in our field or subject, but leadership is altogether a totally different ballgame.

And there are many ways in which we can totally mess things up. One sure-shot way is to brag about our experience in the field, asking our subordinates to suggest new ideas.

We assume that we are encouraging the subordinates, but it is not so. Such a blatant show of I-am-better-than-you never works. Everyone has a part to play in the larger picture; no one is better or worse than the other. At the end of the day, it is the entire team's effort that brings forth the result.

We must remember, at all times, that every person is different. We cannot and should not treat them the same. Parents are exposed to this universal truth the moment they have their second child. They realize it soon enough—that whatever child-rearing tips they learnt while bringing up their firstborn are absolutely useless for bringing up their second. In an organization, too, each person has to be handled differently. The mess-up happens when, in order to be fair to all, we treat them in the same way.

We need to divert our attention from our subordinates and focus on ourselves—on setting the right example for them to follow. If we show up late or lose temper easily, can we really expect our subordinates to be punctual and tolerant? If we start our day with a cup of coffee, can we tell our children that it's bad for them?

The qualities that we want our subordinates to have should be projected through our own behaviour. When we do so, the likelihood of these qualities getting rubbed off on our subordinates is very high. Remember the old adage, 'we earn respect only through our behaviour; not by commanding it'. Well, it holds true in every situation, in every relationship.

As a leader, it is important to set the right example in terms of our own behaviour, just as Krishna did before announcing the war in the Mahabharata.

Let us see how he did that.

The war had not been declared yet, though it was imminent from the way the relationship between the Kauravas and Pandavas was souring by the day.

The Pandavas had completed their 12 years of exile, plus the thirteenth year of living incognito. They took up residence in Upaplavya, close to Viratnagar, for the marriage of Arjun's son Abhimanyu with Viratnagar's princess Uttara.

As it happens in weddings, all the relatives from both sides congregated at the venue. Abhimanyu's mother was Subhadra, Krishna's sister, so her entire clan came from Dwarka. So did Draupadi's, from Panchal. And as it also happens in weddings, the elders sat together and conferred. They discussed the past, the present and the future of their own families as well the newly forged relationships.

Krishna and his brother Balaram, King Drupad and his sons Shikhandi and Drishtadyumna, and many other kings and noblemen sat down to discuss what the Pandavas should do after the wedding celebrations were concluded. It must be mentioned here that the Pandavas had lost their kingdom to their cousins, the Kauravas, in a gambling game. So now they had no place to call home, hence the import of the discussion.

Krishna addressed the gathering, 'You all know how Yudhishthir was cheated in the game and lost everything to the Kauravas. You also know that the Pandavas have fulfilled their pledge of a humiliating exile. Now think well and advise what should be the next step for Yudhishthir. He wants only what is fair, nothing more, nothing less. We do not know Duryodhan's plans as yet. I feel that Yudhishthir should send an emissary to Duryodhan to ask for half their kingdom.'

Balaram seconded Krishna's suggestion, but added his own. He said, 'Yudhishthir knew what he was doing when he gambled his kingdom away. The Kauravas were cheating, but then Yudhishthir did not stop when he was asked to do so by his own family. Now, though he has fulfilled his pledge of exile, it only gives him personal freedom. It does not give him any right over the kingdom that he has lost. So, he can only request Duryodhan, not demand anything. This fact should be kept in mind.'

This was an important observation. But there were rebuttals to this. The other kings felt that Yudhishthir had been conned into losing; so he was not at fault. They said that a polite request should be sent, but at the same time, tentative preparations for war should also be undertaken—at least theoretically, if not practically.

The elders started discussing, and finally reached the conclusion that the emissary to be sent to Duryodhan should be intelligent and tactful. He should be able to impress all the other elders too, and not just Duryodhan, with his peaceful intentions. The idea was that a peaceful settlement should be reached and war should be avoided, if possible.

A brahmin was deputed as the Pandavas' emissary. Brahmins in those days were the epitome of intelligence, education, tact, calmness and gentleness, as opposed to the kshatriyas, who were the ruling class and aggressive by nature.

Plan of action sorted, Krishna went back to Dwarka and so did the other guests, to their respective kingdoms.

The brahmin-diplomat was sent to Hastinapur on the peace mission.

Travelling took a lot of time in those days. So, while the peace emissary took his time to reach his destination, the Pandavas set about garnering support for their cause. Suddenly there was a lot of activity. The Kauravas' spies alerted them, so they also started preparing for the imminent war.

Krishna was related to the Kauravas as well as the Pandavas. So, as a part of their preparation, Arjun from the Pandava family and Duryodhan from the Kaurava family rushed to meet him in Dwarka. When they reached his house, Krishna was sleeping. Duryodhan waited at his bedside, while Arjun stood at Krishna's feet. When Krishna awoke, he asked the cousins the reason for their visit.

Duryodhan blurted out that war between the Kauravas and the Pandavas seemed imminent and they needed Krishna's support. He also pointed out that since he was there first, he should be allowed to ask for the favour first. But Krishna dismissed that, saying that he saw Arjun first, so who was there first became a matter of perspective. He wanted to give the younger one the first pick. The options were his huge army on one side, and he himself on the other. He also emphasized that he would not pick up any arms in the war.

Krishna then asked Arjun what he wanted. Arjun immediately asked for the unarmed Krishna to support him in the war. Duryodhan, of course, was happy receiving Krishna's huge army to fight for him.

So, here the situation became very clear. In the case of a war, Krishna would be on the side of the Pandavas, which for the Kauravas was the enemy's side.

Coming back to the peace emissary. The man went and

tried to reason with the elders of the Kaurava clan. He tried explaining that since the Pandavas' father and the Kauravas' father were both sons of the same father, they held equal claims to their father's kingdom.

But then, friends of Duryodhan, like Karna, objected to this idea. They felt that since Yudhishthir had lost his kingdom in a game of dice, claiming it back was out of the question. He should beg for it and then take whatever the Kauravas decided to give him in charity.

Since this debate seemed unending, Bheeshma, the patriarch of the Kuru clan, told the Pandavas' peace emissary to go back. He said that they would send their own envoy, Sanjay, with their offer.

Sanjay went and told the Pandavas that the Kauravas did not wish to part with any part of their kingdom. But at the same time, he told the Pandavas the futility of indulging in warfare, as it would destroy everything.

This was purely a one-sided deal.

Yudhishthir explained to Sanjay that the Pandavas were not interested in war, but were not afraid of it either. Their needs were limited. Five small villages, one per Pandava brother, would suffice. Then he turned to Krishna to ask him to take the final call. 'Krishna is the wisest one of all. We would happily follow his advice on this matter,' he added.

At the very outset, Krishna said that he was related to both families and wished the best for both of them. He declared that he himself would go and meet the Kauravas as the Pandavas' envoy and ask them to choose between peace and war.

The Pandavas and everyone else dissuaded Krishna from

going into the enemy's camp, as that was what it actually was. But Krishna believed in leading by example. He wanted to show that he was not scared of the enemy. The sending of peace emissaries back and forth was not resulting in any solution to the problem at hand. It was time for the leader to take up the cudgels. The decision had to be taken on site.

Krishna went, without any bodyguards, without any weapons, to meet the Kaurava leaders. As expected, there was an attempt on his life, but Krishna was unfazed. At least this exercise of his would result in a concrete answer, which it did. The Kauravas refused to give even the tiniest piece of land to the Pandavas. They were ready to fight and kill.

Krishna declared the war of Mahabharata.

Right through his life, Krishna never lost his cool. His behaviour was always impeccable and above board. This quality of his, coupled with his wisdom, made him a natural leader of people. Not only his own clan and friends, but people from across the country sought his advice.

Alexander the Great aptly said, 'An army of sheep led by a lion is better than an army of lions led by a sheep.'

We can change other people's behaviour by changing our own. Our own internal philosophy about how to treat people drives our behaviour. So we need to work on that.

Three basic behavioural habits that we need to inculcate in ourselves are:

1. Starting with supportive statements
2. Being present
3. Being transparent

Starting with supportive statements: As parents we have always used this approach with our children. Before teaching a new skill, we start by encouraging them. We always say, 'This is easy, I know you can do it!' be it their first swimming, cycling or driving lesson. We are right next to them while they are learning the new skill. This gives them a sense of security that we are there to save them from any mishap. It also instils self-confidence in them, seeing that their parent has confidence in them. Though the Pandavas were fewer in number than the Kauravas, five against hundred, Krishna always told them that they could win any war.

Being present: Harassment by clients or customers is very common in the corporate world, as in any profession that entails public dealing. A good boss would stand up for his team against the harassment. Privately, we can discuss the issue and plan the future course of action, but publicly, we need to show our solidarity with our subordinates. They should not be made to feel hemmed in. At the end of the day, it's all teamwork, where each member supports the other—and this includes their leader too. Krishna was present with the Pandavas right through the long war of Mahabharata. Though he did not fight himself, his presence in the battlefield was enough to give strength to the Pandava army.

Being transparent: This comes with a rider. It is important to share what frustrates us or what makes us happy, in terms of the overall performance of the organization. It is also important to share our beliefs and to remember that it's not just numbers that make an organization grow. But then, we have to be wise about when and how transparent we are. It is important for our subordinates to see our human sides, but without us divulging any strategies. Krishna knew all the time that neither Duryodhan nor the Pandava brothers would yield. The war had to happen, and he would support the Pandavas in winning it. And they won it too. Yet, all the time, Krishna maintained that war was not the right option. He told both the families how war would destroy them. In fact, he went to the Kauravas as a peacemaker.

What we see here is how Krishna turned out to be a brilliant strategist for the Pandavas.

Setting our internal philosophy at the right frequency, with the help of the behavioural habits mentioned above, will win us half the battle. Let us see what it takes to win the rest.

These six behavioural actions will do the trick:

1. Trusting our team
2. Asking for feedback
3. Avoiding favouritism
4. Acknowledging our limitations
5. Sticking to our commitments
6. Being consistent

Trusting our team: Trust is a two-way process. For someone to trust us, we need to trust them first. There can be no leadership without trust. Our subordinates should not hesitate to share their thoughts with us for fear of judgment. We must give credit to people for their contributions. This motivates them to perform even better. And if something goes wrong, we must acknowledge that it happened under our watch. After all, the leader holds the ultimate responsibility. We should never ever throw our team or any subordinate under the bus.

Asking for feedback: It is very important to have regular feedback sessions, especially after the completion of a project, whether successful or unsuccessful. Discussing where and how we made mistakes in a project is crucial to the execution of future projects. This is a learning exercise, which I am sure must happen in most, if not all, organizations. The role of the leader here is to listen. Listening with an open mind is a great learning experience for the leader as well as the team. It not only helps the leader to make the team perform better next time, but also helps everyone to grow professionally.

In author Mary D. Poole's words, 'Leadership should be more participative than directive, more enabling than performing.'

Avoiding favouritism: Favouritism kills the team spirit. Everyone should be treated fairly. We should have the same set of expectations for everyone. In fact, we should sit with the team to chart out the team rules, setting clear expectations, roles, responsibilities and deliverables for each member. This exercise also helps later in the performance reviews.

Acknowledging our limitations: No one is perfect. And acknowledging one's limitations is not a sign of weakness. Only after accepting and acknowledging our limitations and mistakes can we hope to work upon them and improve ourselves. In any organization, the leader is not expected to be perfect. So if we acknowledge our limitations, we would hire appropriately to supplement that gap. After all, the bottom line remains that the task has to be done effectively to get the desired outcome.

'If you can't swallow your pride, you can't lead. Even

the highest mountain has animals that step on it,' said Jack Weatherford, the great anthropologist.

Sticking to our commitments: Keeping our word is the first step to acquiring trust. As we expect our subordinates to commit to only what they can deliver, so should we expect from ourselves. We should commit according to our capacity and then stick to our commitment, come hell or high water.

Being consistent: This is the showstopper of all the behavioural actions. It is the key to great leadership. Lack of consistency in a leader creates uncertainty and distrust, apart from frustration, in the subordinates. The leader has to be as consistent as the pole star. Mood swings, etc. have no place in leadership.

Leaders who do not walk the talk lose the trust of their subordinates. If we want our subordinates to behave in a certain way, then we have to set the ball rolling ourselves. We should not ask anyone to do what we would not do ourselves.

Intelligent workers are not satisfied by the tokenism of rewards. They seek, apart from a sense of fulfilment in their work, an alignment with their leader. In order to create a sustainable and positive workplace culture, we need to make our subordinates feel safe and supported. We need to give them respect and trust in order to get the same from them. Trust leads to loyalty. And loyalty leads people to do their best for the organization, and for us.

What more does a leader need?

Krishna's approach to leadership clearly shows that leadership indeed is not just a title, but a behaviour.

2.

Krishna on Power

Power is the ability to help others.

The dictionary defines power to be a person's capacity or ability to direct or influence the behaviour of other people or course of events.

Power is derived from leadership, and it leads to leadership. Both are inextricably linked.

What is leadership? It is the ability to inspire people to follow instructions voluntarily, instead of controlling them through the use of any kind of power.

Good leaders use their power judiciously, as abuse or misuse of power is the easiest thing to do.

When we say that power is the ability to help others, it also means that it is the ability to harm others. And that is exactly what happens when a leader misuses power; he becomes a bully. He undermines, intimidates, degrades and even humiliates his subordinates. Such organizations end up having a toxic, insecurity-based culture, with high rates of absenteeism and employee turnover.

Let us see what the most commonly observed instances of misuse or abuse of power are (there are quite a few).

Playing favourites is very common, as some bosses love

to have their egos pampered regularly. Retaliating against anyone who does not agree with them is quite typical too. Such bosses naturally discourage questions with their intimidating attitude.

Then there are those bosses who can't stop showing off their affluence and keep dropping names. They project that their employees are lucky to be working in their organization, and more so, with them.

Another type is the boss who keeps tabs on the comings and goings of the subordinates: one who firmly believes that if we are not in the office, we must be having fun somewhere else. Sounds familiar?

Performance review and appraisal time becomes the most stressful time of the year in organizations where the boss either threatens his subordinates, or worse, takes revenge by not giving them the increments or promotions they deserve.

The same power play happens at home too. Parents reward or punish their children based on their academic performance. Many children are unable to handle the pressures of expectations and the results are disastrous.

As can be seen from the above examples, the wrong use of power can demoralize, whereas the right use motivates people.

Krishna was powerful, and like others before and after his time, he could also have misused his power. But he did not. He was much loved because he used his power to help the people of his village, and eventually the whole country.

One fine morning, young Krishna and his cowherd friends took their cattle to graze near River Yamuna. Some of them went deeper into the nearby thicket of trees. After some time, Krishna realized that the boys were missing. Neither the cows nor the cowherds had returned.

Krishna went to investigate and discovered the boys lying senseless on the riverbank. There were marks of snakebite on them. The cows also seemed dead. It was obviously the job of a poisonous snake. Krishna looked up and saw that the trees and plants overlooking the river at that point were dead and shrivelled up. He realized that a powerful venomous snake must be living in those waters. And since the river water was the lifeline of the villages and towns along its bank, it was imperative to keep it clean.

They young and agile Krishna climbed up a tree and looked around to survey the damage. He saw a substantial area affected by the poison. The poisonous fumes emanating from the water were even killing the birds flying over it. The problem was quite serious, and corrective action had to be taken fast. Krishna had to help his people. He had to kill the source of this poison.

Krishna dived straight into the river from the tree.

Meanwhile, after following him and seeing the dead cows and cowherds, his friends had fetched the villagers. Everyone watched in horror as Krishna dived into the dark, poisonous waters.

The deadly snake was the multi-hooded Kaaliya. His sleep was disturbed by the splash that Krishna made. This was very unusual, as normally, people were scared of Kaaliya and stayed away from him. It was unfortunate that the cows and the cowherds had wandered to his side of the river and could not survive. But who was this foolish creature, who even after seeing the dead boys and cattle, had jumped into his territory?

Not only Kaaliya, but his family, wives and children also wondered at the intrusion. And when they saw that the intruder was a young boy, they dismissed him, assuming that he would also meet the same fate as his cowherd friends.

Krishna began to splash about in the water, the poison not affecting him at all. Kaaliya was irritated at the audacity of the young boy and displayed his fangs with a loud hiss. His own snake-family cowered in fear, but not Krishna. He laughed at the huge snake and egged him to attack, which he did.

Kaaliya grabbed Krishna in a tight coil. His plan was to squeeze the life out the young boy, but the reverse happened. Krishna breathed in and expanded his body to the extent that Kaaliya was in pain and had to loosen his grip.

Krishna slipped out of the snake's coils and started swimming swiftly around him in circles. He was swimming at such speed that Kaaliya, trying to grab him, actually became tired and dizzy.

In frustration, Kaaliya stood up with his multiple hoods bobbing above the water. The people watching from the riverbank screamed in fear at the sight of this huge, poisonous, angry snake. But then, there was a twist.

Dancing on top of the hoods was a smiling Krishna. Kaaliya's wives and other family members also popped out of the river to watch. It was quite an unusual sight.

Krishna's dancing feet were actually trampling the great snake's heads, till he couldn't take it any more and begged for mercy. Kaaliya's wives also requested that their husband be spared.

Krishna agreed on the condition that Kaaliya, with his entire clan, should leave the river and move far away to the ocean. Kaaliya and his family quickly agreed, apologized, and left the place for good. Once that happened, the river was clean again.

This was not the only time Krishna helped the people of his village. He had supernatural powers. He did not flaunt them. But he used them every time there was a crisis or someone was in trouble.

He could not allow his villagers, their cattle or their crop to die because of poisonous water. So he had to take drastic action. He could have easily killed the snake, but because Kaaliya was repentant and promised to go far away, a compassionate Krishna spared his life. Compromises always work out, don't they!

It is believed that when the level of evil overshoots the level of good in the world, there is a lot of chaos, turmoil and unrest. At such a moment, divine power comes down to help in human form. One such form is Krishna.

With the divine power at his disposal, Krishna could have destroyed all the evil in the world in a jiffy. He did not do that. Why? He wanted to teach the humans certain lessons about life, about living in harmony with each other. So, instead of clicking his fingers and waving around his flute or magic wand, Krishna showed that he was a doer. He did things that were lessons to those who witnessed them.

He helped his villagers get rid of superstitious beliefs of praying to Indra by proving that their own Mount Govardhan was more useful than any god. When the giant python-demon Aghasur swallowed his friends and him, Krishna went into his windpipe and inflated himself, choking the python to death and saving his friends.

There is another incident from his childhood. Once Krishna saw a poor fruit seller. He had no money to buy the fruits but wanted to help the poor lady. Looking around he saw some grains drying outside a house. He picked up a handful of grains and went to the fruit-lady. She was poor but very kind. She knew that little Krishna would not be having any money, so she offered the fruits to him as a gift. Krishna refused and said that he would like to pay with the grains that he held in his little palm. The fruit seller smiled and agreed to the deal, giving Krishna a bunch of fruits in return for a fistful of grains. Imagine her surprise when the lady reached home and saw that instead of grains, her fruit basket had gold coins underneath the fruits.

Helping a person at their level, through supernatural or any other kind of power, generates love. Whereas using only supernatural power generates awe. The fruit seller was happy to see the little boy trying to help her by buying her fruits with grains. Of course, discovering gold coins instead was the cherry on the cake—in this case, cake on the cherry! The love and gratitude Krishna generated with his action was way more than the awe he would have generated by magically converting her fruits into coins.

As leaders we need to help our subordinates by being with them when they are stuck with a problem. That way, they will learn and grow, and so will the organization. If we just solve their problems through other means, then every task will become a problem. The need for a team would be redundant. There would be no enterprise, only trading.

An effective leader creates a vision and uses his power to motivate his team to work towards achieving this vision.

Every leader follows his own style of leadership, but they all use one or more of these four leadership powers:

1. Legitimate power
2. Expert power
3. Reward and punishment power
4. Charismatic power

Legitimate power: This power is the official power, which is part of the designation that the leader holds. A simple example would be the various levels of managers: area manager, zone manager, country manager, general manager, etc. They follow a hierarchy, though that does not necessarily mean that the leader is good. It is just the designation that is being followed here.

Expert power: This power is related to our expertise in a subject, which comes from years of experience. It can also be related to our knowledge base. Knowing more than the others is always helpful as a source of power. In some situations, it may even supersede the legitimately powerful leader. This kind of power remains till another expert or knowledgeable person comes into the field.

Reward and punishment power: This power comes with the authority of the position held. Certain positions have the power to promote or reward a worthy subordinate. A reward can be used effectively as a motivator, but can result in distraction as well. The flip side of this is the authority to punish, which typically translates into threat of termination for failure to comply. As can be imagined, it is not very popular.

Charismatic power: This is what the celebrities have—the power to influence people. It is a kind of reverence that the subordinates feel for their leader. They admire him and follow him. It is literally the case of the leader leading by example. Personal magnetism has a huge role to play in such leaders.

Krishna did not hold any specific legitimate designation, like 'king'. He was just the leader of the Yadavas. He was certainly knowledgeable and had the power to reward and punish. As for being charismatic, there is no doubt about that, seeing the following he still has today.

John C. Maxwell, the American thinker on leadership, has expressed it beautifully: 'Leadership is the power of one harnessing the power of many.'

Harnessing is the keyword here. It means 'making productive use of'. And that happens when the leader is helpful, because in helping others he is helping the organization and ultimately himself.

And that, according to Krishna, is the true power.

3.

Krishna on Strategy

Strategy is about choosing what not to do.

A strategy is a plan of action designed to achieve a goal, also called a game plan by some. In an organization, strategies take into account the probable behaviour of clients or customers. The idea is to minimize the competitor's strength and maximize our own.

In life too, that is how a strategy works. It bridges the gap between what we have or where we are and what we want or where we want to be. In our day-to-day lives, too, we plan to buy property or bigger vehicles; we save for our children's weddings or their education abroad. The game plan here is to find out how much fund we need and in how little time, and how to acquire them.

As we run our lives, so we run an organization. We are aware that in life, things may not always go as planned; savings may have to be diverted for an unexpected expenditure like a medical emergency. Similar things can happen in an organization.

Preparing a strategy requires foresight. And it doesn't end there. Implementing it is another story altogether. The best of strategies can fail if the people executing it are not committed enough. So, for a strategy to be successful, the strategist must see it through its execution.

Other than lack of commitment, the reasons for the failure of a strategy could be many. The most obvious ones would be if the strategy itself is not doable, if the goals are unrealistic and if the resources are insufficient. The other, very commonly seen reason for a strategy's failure is lack of awareness or understanding of the environment. The environment is always dynamic, and the strategists as well as the implementers have to be acutely aware of the environmental dynamics and be open to change.

Some strategies are not strategies at all; they are goals or the organization's priorities and choices. For example, 'We want to be number one in the market,' is not a strategy but a goal. It just tells us where we want to be, but not how we will reach there. For that, we need a strategy. 'We want to increase our global presence,' is again a priority, but not a strategy.

In a standard scenario, the strategist would do a SWOT (strengths, weaknesses, opportunities, threats) analysis and plan a strategy that optimally utilizes the strengths, minimizes the weaknesses, uses all the available opportunities and is aware of the threats.

What is missing? There are plenty of things 'to do', but what is 'not to do'?

There are choices to be made while planning a strategy or a course of action. 'What not to do' is also an important part of planning. A simplistic example would be a cross-country road trip. When driving to our destination, we plan the route map and keep in mind which roads not to take to avoid jams and delays.

American President Donald Trump is probably the most successful and extraordinary business entrepreneur in the world. He says, 'Experience taught me a few things. One is to listen to your gut, no matter how good something sounds on paper. The second is that you're generally better off sticking to what you know. And the third is that sometimes your best investments are the ones you don't make.' He also says, 'Part of being a winner is knowing when enough is enough. Sometimes you have to give up the fight and walk away, and move on to something more productive.'

This is where we come to Krishna. It can be safely said that the Pandavas could not have won the war of Mahabharata if Krishna was not on their side.

Krishna was a peace-loving person. He was always against war and tried to talk the Kauravas out of it too. But as we know, the war did happen.

Let us go back to the incident of when the two cousins Duryodhan and Arjun reached Krishna's house to seek his help. It was not a declaration of war then, it was just preparation for the eventuality. But then, Krishna had foresight. He knew that war was certain and he wanted the Pandavas to win.

Krishna was related to both the cousins, but he trusted Arjun more. He did not want to take the risk of Duryodhan asking for his favour first. So he devised the strategy of 'younger ones should be asked first', which seemed pretty fair and made Arjun the first recipient of his favour.

Krishna and Arjun were more friends than relatives. This knowledge gave Krishna the confidence to predict that Arjun would prefer to have him on the Pandavas' side rather than his army. To drive the point home, he emphasized that he would not pick up arms in the war. Krishna was a great warrior himself, but of what use would that be if he did not fight on the battlefield? So Duryodhan thought, and was happy to get Krishna's army to support him in the upcoming war.

Not choosing to fight was the most brilliant strategy of Krishna, and it gave him what he wanted. The Pandavas won the great war of Mahabharata. Krishna's vision of this country being ruled by the righteous Yudhishthir was fulfilled.

Arjun was also smart. He requested Krishna to be his charioteer, to which the latter agreed. In this way, Krishna and Arjun made a formidable team on the battlefield.

Krishna not only guided Arjun's chariot, but also guided him. If he had taken up arms, Krishna would have been busy saving himself from the fierce Kaurava warriors. He could not have helped Arjun or any other Pandavas in the war.

So, Krishna's strategy of not picking up arms in the war kept him free to advise Arjun and his brothers. Though he was not the commander-in-chief of the Pandava army, Krishna still led them to victory.

The Pandava forces were far fewer than the Kauravas. But they had this brilliant strategist in Krishna, who advised them on how to maximize the use of their strengths, minimize their weaknesses, utilize every opportunity that came their way, and foresee the threats in order to demolish them before they could cause any harm. That is SWOT for you!

Krishna led the Pandavas with his advice right from the first day of the war. He boosted their morale every step of the way. Not just Arjun, but the entire Pandava army took his guidance.

On the first day of the Mahabharata war, the Pandava forces suffered heavy losses because of the Kuru clan's patriarch, and granduncle of the Kauravas and Pandavas, Bheeshma Pitamah. The Pandava brothers sought Krishna's advice. He told them not to worry, as Bheeshma was destined to die because of Draupadi's brother Shikhandi.

On the second day, Arjun vowed to kill Bheeshma. Both fought valiantly but Bheeshma had to leave in the middle to rescue his army at another part of the battlefield. Since the Pandavas performed well in the war that day, Arjun became a little complacent.

The war continued. Arjun somehow managed to avoid killing his granduncle.

On the ninth day, while driving his chariot into the battlefield, Krishna reminded Arjun of his vow. Arjun confronted Bheeshma again. This time, somehow, Arjun's heart was not in the combat. He was just responding to Bheeshma's arrows and not attacking him. This made Krishna angry. He said, 'I can't stand this any longer, Arjun. I will kill Bheeshma, if you don't do it!' and he dropped the reins and jumped off the chariot. He then rushed towards Bheeshma with his Sudarshan Chakra spinning on his finger.

Bheeshma bowed to Krishna in reverence and said, 'I would be happy to be slain by you Krishna, as I would then attain heaven and eternal peace.'

Arjun was embarrassed. He did not want Krishna to break his vow and pick up arms. He ran after Krishna to stop him. 'Please do not lose your patience with me, my friend. I promise not to flinch any more.' Unfortunately, it was evening, and the battle for the day was declared over.

Those days the wars were fought within a time frame, and with great discipline. In fact, after war hours, the enemies would even catch up with each other over refreshments.

Krishna's strategy of provoking Arjun had worked. On the tenth day of the battle, he placed Shikhandi strategically in front of Arjun and told them to attack Bheeshma.

Krishna knew that Bheeshma would not attack or respond to Shikhandi's arrows as the later was born a woman and had only changed into a man later in life. Bheeshma would never attack a woman. So, Shikhandi acted as an impenetrable shield for Arjun. Bheeshma fell at the combined onslaught of Arjun and Shikhandi, because he could not fight back. It was a day of major victory for the Pandavas.

There were many occasions during the battle when Krishna, using his amazing driving skills, led as well as protected Arjun. He was a formidable warrior himself, but fighting in the war alongside the Pandavas like any other warrior would have been a waste. Krishna was more useful as a strategist.

Not only Bheeshma, but other Kaurava stalwarts were also felled using Krishna's strategies.

Drona was another powerful army-chief of the Kauravas. Drishtadyumna, Draupadi's brother, had vowed to kill him, but it did not seem possible in a straight war. A strategy was needed. Krishna came up with an idea. He said, 'If Drona is told that his son Ashwatthama has been killed in the battle, he will drop his weapons in sorrow. And that is when you can kill him.' So an elephant named Ashwatthama was killed and Drona was informed, 'Ashwatthama has been killed.' It was not a blatant lie, and it did the trick. Drona dropped his weapons and was killed by Drishtadyumna.

The next victim of Krishna's strategy was Karna, Arjun's arch-rival. Soon they faced each other in fierce combat. Unfortunately, the left wheel of Karna's chariot got stuck in the mud. He had to get down to free it. According to the rules of the war, Arjun was not supposed to strike his opponent until his vehicle was on the move again. Karna reminded Arjun that he was obligated to spare him while he was retrieving the wheel of his chariot.

But how could Krishna let go of this golden opportunity! He chided Karna for talking of obligations. He reminded him of the times Karna had supported his friend Duryodhan in committing sinful activities against the Pandavas. Krishna questioned Karna's sense of fair play when a bunch of armed Kaurava warriors, including him, had killed an unarmed Abhimanyu. The mention of his son angered Arjun so much that he shot and killed Karna, while he was still trying to pull out his chariot's wheel from the mud. Denouncing Karna was Krishna's strategy to demoralize him and provoke Arjun into action.

All through the great battle of Mahabharata, it can be seen how useful Krishna was to the Pandavas, even though he never picked up any arms. His biggest strategy was to choose not to fight himself.

Typically, the three key features needed for strategic planning are:

1. Knowledge of the goal/s
2. Knowledge of the uncertainty of events
3. Knowledge of the likely and actual behaviour of others

Knowledge of the goal/s: Krishna's goal was to make the Pandavas win the war of Mahabharata.

Knowledge of the uncertainty of events: A war is an uncertain event on a day-to-day basis.

Knowledge of the likely and actual behaviour of others: Right from the outset, Krishna manipulated Duryodhan into taking his army and feeling happy about it. This he did by choosing not to fight in the battle and hence making Duryodhan think that an armed army would be a much better choice than an unarmed Krishna. Then knowing fully well how Arjun would behave, Krishna provoked him into killing Bheeshma and Karna. In the same way, knowing how Drona was likely to behave on getting the news of his son's death, he got the Pandavas to play that trick on him, leading to his death.

It can be seen that strategic management is all about integrating and utilizing the available resources to meet the objective, along with planning for both predictable and unforeseeable contingencies. This is true for all organizations as well as individuals.

The three vital components of a strategy are:

1. Goal
2. Mission
3. Vision

Goal: A goal is the desired future state or objective that the organization wants to achieve. It should be precise and realistic. Goals can be short term or long term, but for both, the strategizing process and components remain the same.

Mission: A mission statement tells us how we will get where we want to be. It should be inspiring and yet feasible.

Vision: A vision statement outlines where we want to be. It should be clear and realistic, and also harmonize with the organization's core values.

Once there is clarity on the objective of the strategy, keeping in mind the three vital components, the strategizing process is accomplished in four steps. They are:

1. Analysis
2. Formulation
3. Implementation
4. Evaluation

Analysis: Collecting and scrutinizing the environmental information is crucial to formulating any strategy. It helps in analysing the internal and external factors influencing the organization.

Formulation: After acquiring complete knowledge of the environment, the next step is to formulate the strategy. It is the process of deciding the best course of action to achieve the organization's goal.

Implementation: Strategy implementation includes designing the organization's structure, developing the decision-making process and managing resources. Implementation implies making the strategy work as intended to achieve the desired goal.

Evaluation: This is the last but very critical part of the strategy management process. It involves appraising the internal and external factors involved in the action as well as measuring the performance. It also outlines corrective or remedial measures, if needed. The evaluation process has to make sure that the strategy and its implementation meet the organizational objectives. If they fall short, then remedial measures have to be designed.

This entire strategizing process is done in a chronological order and is interconnected.

A strategy is about making hard choices. We have to step out of our comfort zone. The objective is not to eliminate risks, but to increase the odds of success. Krishna was not a charioteer, but he stepped out of his comfort zone and became one.

A true strategy involves a clear set of choices that define what we are going to do and what we are not. Krishna chose to become Arjun's charioteer and also chose not to pick up arms and fight in the war.

Krishna indeed was a strategist par excellence.

4.

Krishna on Team Building

Collaboration divides the task and multiplies the success.

Two or more people working together constitute a team. In the organizational context, we can rephrase it to say, a team is two or more people working together to achieve a common goal.

The best examples of teams are seen in sports. Selection, training and guiding the team to give their best to achieve the target are all part of the team-building exercise. At a micro level, we can see team building in a family of two or more children; how the children team up to get what they want from their parents. The leader is not necessarily the eldest child, it's mostly the one who is most manipulative and knows how to make the parents agree to their demands.

But then, teams are known to fail. They may fail due to multiple reasons like lack of resources or lack of proper planning, but the main reason is mostly lack of proper collaboration between the team members.

Team failure leads to loss of business in an organization. Hence, team building becomes a very important aspect of leadership. In fact, it is one of the pillars of organizational development.

The most common reasons behind any team's failure are:

1. Lack of proper leadership
2. Lack of well-defined goal/s
3. Lack of training
4. Lack of incentive
5. Fear of failure
6. Strengths and weaknesses of members
7. Presence of disruptive members
8. Lack of communication

Lack of proper leadership: This is the first and the most basic reason for a team's failure. Every team needs to have a leader who maps out the goal, sets expectations and keeps the team focussed. The leader is needed to keep the team motivated, continue the morale-boosting exercise regularly, and at the same time, maintain discipline and hold the team members accountable for their performance.

Lack of well-defined goal/s: A well-defined goal is important for anyone to grow in life. Not only does the team need a goal to work towards, the team members also need their individual goals charted out for them. But, it has to be kept in mind that collaboration has to be promoted here, not competition.

Lack of training: When we fail to upgrade our team regularly, how can we expect them to carry out jobs that they are not trained to do? It is important to have training programmes in the organization if we want to be successful. The world out there is forever changing and growing, technologies evolve on a daily basis, and we need to be up-to-date if we want to compete and succeed.

Lack of incentive: At times, the team members do not feel personally connected to the organization's goal. It is important for each team member to feel involved in the task and the big picture ahead. A word of acknowledgment and appreciation in public does wonders to boost the morale of any team member. And that itself can act as an incentive.

Fear of failure: Sometimes an organization has very strict penalties for defaulters and that affects the efficiency of team members negatively. They work under pressure and are unable to give their best. They are not bothered about winning, as the fear of losing is much greater.

Strengths and weaknesses of members: Each team member is different in what and how much they can contribute to the task at hand. It is imperative to make judicious use of the strengths and weaknesses of the team to get the best out of the collective effort.

Presence of disruptive members: There is always a disruptive member in the team, who loves to follow a different path. It is important to identify and harness that person's strengths. If they are unable to follow the path, then they should be relieved of their tasks. There is no point in wasting anyone's energy on trying to set things right when they can't be.

Lack of communication: This happens when the team members do not meet regularly or often enough to resolve their queries or grievances. For a smooth workflow, the team members have to be in sync with each other. They should have a platform or forum to clear up any issues that they might have with the fellow members, their leader, or even the organization itself.

Team building is clearly a vital aspect of effective leadership.

Much before the war of Mahabharata, the Kauravas and Pandavas were living together in Hastinapur, though not peacefully. There was a lot of sibling rivalry amongst the cousins. Till they were children, the rivalry was manageable. Once they had grown up to become young men, the rivalry took a serious turn. The eldest Pandava, Yudhishthir's popularity was increasing day by day. Duryodhan, the eldest of the Kauravas, did not appreciate it at all. So much so, that along with his brothers, he decided to get rid of the Pandavas.

The plan was to get a lac palace built for the Pandavas in a nearby town and send them to live there. And once they settled down, the palace was to be set on fire. Lac being extremely inflammable, would burn in no time, killing the inhabitants trapped inside. Since the palace would be far away from them, the Kauravas would be above suspicion. The plan looked foolproof, but it wasn't.

It turned out that one of the well-wishers of the Pandavas alerted them about the plan and they sneaked out of the lac palace and were saved from the blaze. Five men and their mother were trapped inside, who had come there for dinner and had stayed back for the night. Unfortunately for them and fortunately for the Pandavas, the charred bodies were assumed to be those of the five Pandava brothers and their mother.

To cut the long story short, the Pandavas wandered in the forests for a long time and ended up getting married to

Princess Draupadi of Panchal. Since now it became public knowledge that the Pandavas were alive, Duryodhan's father, King Dhritarashtra had to call them back to Hastinapur. But, instead of asking them to live in the main palace, like they used to, the king gave the Pandavas a wasteland called Khandavprastha.

The Pandavas worked hard and converted that deserted place into a flourishing township. The place was now called Indraprastha and it was growing fast. Yudhishthir became the king of this new kingdom. He was a fair ruler. There was plenty for all. Everyone was happy and Yudhishthir's fame spread far and wide.

The kings of neighbouring kingdoms started visiting King Yudhishthir in Indraprastha, to pay their respects. This was deemed as an understanding that they would support him in case of need. Slowly, the number of kings showing support increased so much that it seemed that Yudhishthir was controlling a major part of the country. But then, it was not official.

In those days, in order to prove that a great many kings were supporting one king, the latter had to conduct a sacrificial ceremony called Rajasuya. All the other kings would attend this ceremony and accept the host king as their emperor. An emperor was akin to the chief executive officer of a company and the king, the regional manager.

Yushishthir's family and friends suggested that he should hold a Rajasuya and declare his supremacy. It seemed a wise course of action, but Yushishthir decided to take Krishna's advice on it.

Krishna knew that Yudhishthir had the potential to be the

emperor of not just an empire of a handful of kingdoms but the entire country, Bharat (the ancient name for the Indian subcontinent). But to rule the entire country he had to have a good team of follower-kings who would do his bidding when need be.

'Jarasandh, the king of Magadh, is a powerful ruler and has eighty-six kings in his prisons. He plans to immolate a hundred kings and is waiting to get hold of fourteen more to reach the number. Killing this king will garner you the support of the kings he has captured. Then it would be the right time to hold Rajasuya and show the entire country your might,' Krishna advised Yudhishthir.

This Jarasandh was such a ferocious king that Krishna himself had lost a three-year-long battle with him and had to leave his town of Mathura and set up his domain further west in Dwarka.

Anyway, it was decided that Krishna's wisdom, Yudhishthir's younger brother Bheem's strength and his other younger brother Arjun's dexterity as an archer should be combined and used against Jarasandh to kill him.

Getting the allegiance of Magadh and the hundred kings in its captivity for Yudhishthir was a huge step towards establishing him as the ruler of the Indian subcontinent. This was a case of team building by Krishna for Yudhishthir. And the goal was set by him much before the battle of Mahabharata. Krishna knew the worth of a good team.

As planned, Krishna went with Arjun and Bheem to Magadh. Dressed as hermits, they tricked Jarasandh into allowing them to enter the palace. Once inside, they told him that they were his enemies and had actually come to fight with him to kill him. Jarasandh chose Bheem for unarmed combat.

Sometimes a small but efficient team can do what a large one cannot. Earlier Krishna lost to the same Jarasandh in the battlefield when he had a huge army as his team. This time around, he gained access into the king's palace in the guise of a hermit, which was convincing because there were just three of them.

Those days, people would strictly adhere to the code of conduct assigned to their caste. So a warrior could not refuse a challenge from another warrior. Three warriors cornered Jarasandh in his own palace; he had to accept the challenge and fight for his life.

A king has his army by his side on the battlefield, which supports and protects him. But in a situation of one-to-one combat, there is no support or protection. A wise Krishna had built his team accordingly.

Jarasandh and Bheem fought for 13 days with no result. They were equally matched in strength. On the fourteenth day, when Jarasandh started showing signs of exhaustion, Krishna gestured to Bheem to take advantage of the situation. It was like a coach suggesting to the players of his team what to do next, as he's the one sitting on the periphery and watching both sides play.

Krishna had already told Bheem how Jarasandh could be killed—by splitting him vertically into two halves. The time had come. Krishna picked up a leaf and tore it into two, vertically. Bheem took the hint and did the same with Jarasandh.

A good leader not only builds a good team, he directs them

well and leads them to achieve the desired goal successfully.

Killing Jarasandh, releasing all the captive kings and installing Jarasandh's son as the king of Magadh, the Pandavas acquired allegiance from all of them. Yudhishthir's kitty of supportive kings increased substantially. Krishna had set him on the path of becoming the emperor of the entire Indian subcontinent in the distant future.

Henry Ford, founder of the Ford Motor Company, has described teamwork aptly thus, 'Coming together is a beginning, keeping together is progress, working together is success.'

Building a team involves four steps:

1. Setting goals
2. Clarifying team members' roles
3. Building effective working relationships
4. Finding solutions to team problems

Setting goals: This has to be the first step, logically. Because, unless we know the goal we are setting out to reach, we cannot know the requirements for it. The selection of a team is dependent on what we want them to achieve.

Clarifying team members' roles: Once the goal is set and the team is selected, the next step is to distribute the roles and responsibilities to each member of the team. It is important for each team member to feel that they are an important part of the collective task. Every member has an individual goal to attain, for the team to attain the collective goal.

Building effective working relationships: If the team members don't get along well with each other, they are unlikely to cooperate. As any kind of friction slows down the movement of a machine, friction among team members also slows down the team. Mutual trust among the team members is important to create strong interpersonal relationships.

Finding solutions to team problems: A team is like a family. It will always have its share of problems, which need to be solved as soon as possible. This depends a lot on the interpersonal relationships and camaraderie of the team members inside and outside the organization. Effective communication is important here, because many problems can be resolved simply by talking.

Going back to Krishna, let us see how he utilized the above four steps in team building.

Yudhishthir wanted his advice on conducting a Rajasuya. Krishna used this to establish his ultimate goal of making Yudhishthir the emperor of Bharat. Goal established; he wanted to build a strong team that had the strength and passion to achieve it. He needed numbers.

Jarasandh had numbers; he was controlling a hundred kingdoms. But those kings were more useful to Yudhishthir. If they could be saved from Jarasandh, they would happily fight for Yudhishthir. Under Jarasandh, they would be fighting under duress, which is not good for morale and does not necessarily lead to success. Krishna decided that Jarasandh should be killed.

At this point, the first problem appeared. Yudhishthir shot down the idea. His contention was that if Krishna's army lost to Jarasandh, how could his army expect to win? A smaller, sharper team was needed to achieve this. Two brothers with different skill-sets were selected, one in wrestling, the other in archery. They trusted their leader Krishna implicitly. The second problem was to get close to Jarasandh. The team resolved this by disguising themselves as hermits.

Finally, when the combat started between Jarasandh and Bheem, Krishna was observing closely. The moment he saw an opportunity, he signalled to Bheem to take action. Since Krishna had told Jarasandh's story to the team members on their way, understanding his hint was easy for Bheem. This is the power of good understanding and communication in creating effective interpersonal bonds among team members.

Jarasandh was killed. Krishna's short-term goal was achieved. He was on his way to the larger one now.

Team building also involves team management, which requires these six skills:

1. Patience
2. Ability to relate
3. Flexibility
4. Trust
5. Ability to listen
6. An open mind

Patience: This is one skill that is useful to us in every situation of our life, leading a team being one of them. We always think we have patience till we lose it when the situation or people get(s) tough. That has to be avoided. Deep breathing helps.

Ability to relate: Any organization is made of people. So understanding other viewpoints is vital in running it smoothly. The best way to relate to others is to imagine ourselves in their shoes and think. Everyone has their own perspective and we need to understand that.

Flexibility: This comes from the ability to relate. If we are able to see where the other person is coming from, we can understand their viewpoint and maybe check out their suggestions. Flexibility, like patience, is required all the time in life. It is the ability to understand that there could be ways other than ours to accomplish the same task; it is the ability to adapt to changing circumstances.

Trust: Trust is an important ingredient of any relationship, so is it between the team leader and the team. We have to trust that our team members have the best interest of the organization at heart.

Ability to listen: This is a very important quality in a leader. A leader should be able to spend time to listen to his team members without interrupting and then think before responding.

An open mind: In order to develop trust and respect in the team members, it is important for their leader to have an open mind. The team members should feel that their viewpoint, feedback and suggestions are valued.

Steve Jobs has put it very beautifully, 'My model for business is the Beatles. They were four guys who kept each other's negative tendencies in check. They balanced each other and the total was greater than the sum of the parts. That's how I see business: Great things in business are never done by one person, they're done by a team of people.'

Krishna collaborated with the Pandavas and successfully got rid of a major roadblock on the way to his goal.

5.

Krishna on Communication

The art of communication is in the art of listening.

Communication, simply put, is the conveying and sharing of ideas and feelings. It is something we do everyday with everyone. It is the core of our society. It is what makes us human.

Communication is more than what we say. It comprises of how we say it and when we say it. It also includes our body language and what we don't say.

Unfortunately, communication is also a skill that is taken for granted most often. We assume that will be able to easily communicate whatever we are thinking to anyone. But most of the times, it is not so. That is where misunderstandings creep up—from miscommunication, ineffective communication or failure of communication.

So what are the reasons behind failure of communication? There are four common causes:

1. Using complicated language
2. Being judgmental
3. Giving unsolicited advice
4. Being inattentive

Using complicated language: This happens when the communicator tries to show his superiority by using unnecessarily difficult words and technical jargon. The best communication happens when the language is kept simple and brief.

Being judgmental: Judging other people by one's own parameters is a very irritating habit of some people. Things like, 'You won't be able to do this' or 'This is something you should have learnt twenty years ago' or 'People from that part of the world always do this' show biases that are very detrimental to communication.

Giving unsolicited advice: Sounds familiar? This is a trap that most people fall into while communicating. They end up giving unasked-for advice. Actually, telling the other person what to do or not to do is the easiest thing to do, isn't it! And it is the most off-putting thing to listen to, too.

Being inattentive: This is the worst thing we can do to anyone. Not making eye contact, looking elsewhere, interrupting the conversation without allowing the other person to put their point across, are some of the commonly committed mistakes. But the king of all the rude and insensitive behaviours is working on a computer or fiddling with the mobile while someone is talking to us.

From the above, we can see why a communication breakdown happens between parents and their children. The children don't like the unsolicited advice from their parents the moment they enter their teens, and they always blame their parents for being judgmental. Parents have constant complaints about their children being inattentive and using strange, unfamiliar language.

Let us see how Krishna fares in the art of communication.

In the story of Mahabharata, Krishna appeared for the first time in Draupadi's marriage in the kingdom of Panchal. It was a contest, where the grooms had to compete for the bride, and the best man would win her. In Princess Draupadi's case, the task was to pierce the eye of a revolving fish hung high above, taking aim only by its reflection in the water at ground level.

King Drupad had invited princes from all across the country to participate in the contest. The Kauravas were present there, as were Krishna, his brother Balaram and other Yadavas from Mathura. The Pandavas were present there in the guise of brahmins. They were on the run, as their cousin Duryodhan was trying to get them killed.

Arjun proved himself to be the best archer in the assembly, as only he could perform the task successfully. This agitated the noblemen present there. They felt that a brahmin should not be allowed to marry a princess. They created a scene and in their anger, tried to attack Arjun. Some even targeted Draupadi, telling her that it would better for her to immolate herself rather than marry a brahmin. The situation was getting ugly.

Bheem, the second of the Pandava brothers, quickly went out and uprooted a large tree. Breaking away and cleaning its branches and leaves, he stood with the tree in his hand like a giant mace. But the assembled people had become quite unruly by now.

This is when Krishna stepped in as a peacemaker and averted the crisis.

He addressed the aggrieved grooms, 'O kings, that man has rightfully won the princess. You must calm down and stop fighting.' He reminded them that being warriors and noblemen, they were required to follow righteousness and stand for justice. Since no rules were broken and the task was successfully achieved, it was only fair that the archer be gracefully declared a winner and Draupadi be married to him.

The assembled people understood Krishna's explanation and calmed down, though not without some envy for the young 'brahmin' winner.

Now, Krishna had recognized Arjun and could have picked up arms and fought with those who were opposing him. Bheem had done that. But Krishna never became aggressive where peaceful means could work. He used his skill of communication; he heard the complaints, the grudges of the angry lot of noblemen. He knew that they were wrong.

Krishna spoke to the noblemen, he reasoned with them, he analysed and explained the entire incident. He convinced them that they were over-reacting and were being unfair. After calming down, the noblemen realized that what Krishna was saying made sense, and they backed off.

Krishna managed to get everyone's attention. They heard him out patiently and accepted whatever he said. That is an example of the brilliant communication skills of an effective leader. As the American presidential speechwriter James Humes says, 'The art of communication is the language of leadership.'

Communication is required to perform the basic functions in an organization, like planning, organizing, leading and controlling. It is the lifeblood of an organization.

Blood transports oxygen and nutrition throughout every cell of our body and transports carbon dioxide and other waste materials, too, from the cells to the excretory organs. In the same way, communication is a means of transport for information, both good and bad.

Communication should always be:

1. Concise
2. Clear
3. Complete

Concise: The information should be precise and concise, expressed in as few words as possible. In communication, less is always more. It registers better. 'Brevity is the soul of wit,' said Shakespeare, but brevity is also the soul of effective communication.

Clear: Apart from brevity, clarity is important in any communication, more so in business communication. Clear and coherent communication is easy to understand and has less chances of being misinterpreted.

Complete: Correct and complete communication leaves no room for doubt. It calls for action. It gives the receiver as much information as they are supposed to receive. Such a communication is indicative of the fact that the leader has complete understanding of his or her thoughts. And this is impactful.

At Draupadi's wedding, Krishna did not get into any discussions with the offended persons. He did not detail the rights of brahmins and kshatriyas (warriors). He was clear in his own understanding of the issue. He knew what had happened and he also knew why the other contenders were upset. He stated the fact to them simply, that Arjun had 'rightfully won' Draupadi. That was the main thing. Once the noblemen accepted that, the rest was easy. The goal was achieved. Unnecessary fight was avoided. Arjun was married to Draupadi.

Every communication has six essential components:

1. Context
2. Sender
3. Message
4. Medium
5. Receiver
6. Reaction

In the above incident from Krishna's life, the context was selection of the right groom for Draupadi. The sender or the communicator was Krishna. The message was that Arjun was the right groom for Draupadi. He had won her rightfully by successfully completing the required task. The medium was oral. Krishna had to stand up and address the gathering. The receiver was the gathering of disgruntled noblemen who did not like the idea of Arjun marrying Draupadi. The reaction was positive. The gathered noblemen understood Krishna's point of view and stopped protesting.

Communication skills like those of Krishna do not happen overnight. They have to be cultivated and nurtured.

There are three skills that make communication effective:

1. Active listening
2. Asking questions
3. Summarizing

Active listening: The best way to understand people is to listen to them. We need to be alert and pay our full attention to the person who is talking to us. On no account should we interrupt the flow of the talker to ask or say anything. All our questions or remarks should be kept for the end. That way the distractions or digressions are avoided. Active listening also includes non-verbal communication that we do by way of eye contact, and gestures—basically our body language. So we need to be aware of our non-verbal communication through our body language. It should not go against the person we are listening to.

Asking questions: This is a very important aspect of communication. To make any communication two-way, we must ask the speaker questions and get into a healthy discussion. This also helps us to detail out the topic and understand it in depth.

Summarizing: This is the final and the most crucial step in communication. Once we have heard what the other person has said, we need to reflect on it and clarify it with our own understanding. Finally, we should summarize it in front of the speaker, so that they may check whether we have received what they are trying to get across.

Effective communication skills are needed not only to communicate our point across and convince the other person, but also to motivate our subordinates. Communication is also a source of information, which is vital to our assessment and decision-making processes.

Communication, as a tool, has the power to create or destroy ideas. It helps in moulding people's attitudes, hence the popularity of using social media as the means to communicate with the masses.

These powerful words from Gilbert Amelio, former CEO of Apple Inc., sum it all up very neatly:

'Developing excellent communication skills is absolutely essential to effective leadership. The leader must be able to share knowledge and ideas to transmit a sense of urgency and enthusiasm to others. If a leader can't get a message across clearly and motivate others to act on it, then having a message doesn't even matter.'

6.

Krishna on Work-Life Balance

The balance is within.

Work-life balance is the term we use to describe the balance that we need to achieve between our time spent at work and that spent on things other than work. It does not mean that the time spent on both should be equal. Also, it is important to remember that work-life balance is different for different people.

We should work to achieve something and we should live happily. So essentially, work-life balance should be a balance between achievement and happiness.

It may sound simple, but it's far from that. We may spend X number of hours at work, technically, but what about the time spent thinking about work or discussing with colleagues? All that construes time spent on work-related activities. The problem is that everything happens so seamlessly that we don't even realize that we are working practically all the time! Our work-life balance gets skewed. And by the time we realize it, it's already too late.

How to avoid that? We must look out for these seven warning signs:

1. Working for long hours

2. Drinking too much coffee or tea
3. Constantly thinking of work
4. Constantly checking emails
5. Not taking any vacation
6. Becoming impatient
7. Having no social life

Working for long hours: This is a silent one. We don't even get to know that we are working for long hours till we actually sit down and calculate. The official working hours are supposed to be eight hours per day or 40 hours per week for a five-day week or 48 hours in a six-day week scenario. But invariably, we start extending this time slowly and the result is that we end up working for 60–70 hours in a week. This is detrimental to our health and predisposes us to type-2 diabetes and heart problems. Fifty hours of work in a week is enough to maintain a work-life balance. Going beyond this causes imbalance and is not advisable.

Drinking too much coffee or tea: This is serious. If we need excessive coffee or tea to pull us through our day, it clearly shows we're not up to it. Either we are putting in more physical hours at work or mental hours while off work. In both the cases, we need to slow down or take a break. Otherwise, soon enough we would be drinking alcohol or taking sleeping pills, which may eventually lead to depression or severe anxiety.

Constantly thinking of work: This becomes a habit. And it's a bad habit when we start doing this at home or any place other than work. Being focused on work while working is a great quality, but we need to know when to switch off our work-brain. If we don't do it, we are likely to burn out faster and fall prey to lifestyle diseases like hypertension.

Constantly checking emails: This is a side effect of smartphones. Our phone is always by our side and checking social media all the time has become a habit already. The emails also pop up, so it becomes difficult to avoid checking them. But then, some people check their emails very frequently, as though they are scared to miss anything important. This habit converts into anxiety. We should understand that we need to work only for a certain number of hours, and so do the other people. They would not and should not expect prompt responses, and so shouldn't we. Checking emails 24x7 stresses out the sender as well as the receiver.

Not taking any vacation: This is also a serious matter. We need to believe in the fact that the organization will not fall apart on our taking a short vacation, though *we* might if we don't take it. Every organization has the provision of leaves and the idea is to avail them to maintain our mental and physical health. If we don't take a break, we're heading towards a major work-life imbalance. Dedication is a good thing, but if we are stressed out, our work suffers and that doesn't help the organization at all. Leaves should be taken to avoid falling sick, rather than falling sick and being forced to take sick leave.

Becoming impatient: This is a red flag indeed. The symptoms of impatience creep up slowly. We start losing temper fast and get provoked easily. Normally, one has enough reserves of patience to handle work as well as life, but when the balance is skewed, the reserves get over fast. We are always on edge, on a short fuse and ready to burst. This is a sure sign leading us to heart problems and stroke. By this stage, our performance may also have dropped, which throws us into a vicious cycle of impatience killing performance, bad performance killing patience, and so on, and finally all this killing us. We need to take a break to break this cycle.

No social life: Social life here does not mean socializing with colleagues. That also has undercurrents of work. The real social life is the time spent with family and friends other than colleagues. If the family is not in town, then weekend breaks to visit them would be a good idea.

Marketing genius Heather Schuck says, 'You will never feel truly satisfied by work until you are satisfied by life.' This is worth pondering over.

Getting distracted once in a while in work due to family issues is not a problem. But, when either one of them—family issues or work issues—starts spilling over the other far too often, then it's time to sit up and set things right.

Krishna had to nudge Arjun out of his off-balance state once in the middle of the battle of Mahabharata. It was on day 13 of the great war.

The Kaurava army-chief Drona had diverted Arjun and Krishna to another part of the battlefield, while he arranged the Kaurava army in a discus formation on the main field.

Those days, wars were fought in dynamic formations of the army to attain the purpose of the day. In the war of Mahabharata, 17 types of formations were used, like heron, crocodile, trident, discus, etc. The discus formation was like a maze and any enemy soldier entering it would be trapped from all sides and be killed.

The Kauravas' discus formation was decimating the Pandava forces at great speed. Arjun knew how to break through this formation, but he was busy at the other end of the battlefield. Pandavas were starting to lose hope, when Arjun's son Abhimanyu offered to break into the formation. He knew how to get in, but didn't know the way out. He needed someone to watch his back. The plan was that Abhimanyu would break into the formation, closely followed by the other Pandavas. They assumed that in numbers they would be able to destroy the formation. But things don't always work out as planned.

Abhimanyu entered the formation, and swiftly, the Kaurava soldiers blocked the entry of any other Pandava soldier. They practically surrounded Abhimanyu from all sides. He fought valiantly, but was killed by a bunch of Kaurava stalwarts, including Drona himself.

The news of his son's death was heartbreaking for Arjun. He burst into tears. Abhimanyu was a young boy, recently married. Arjun worried about his young wife, who was pregnant; he worried about Subhadra, Abhimanyu's mother. He did not know how he could possibly comfort them. How can a mother and a wife be comforted when such tragedy befalls them? Arjun sank into despair.

When Krishna saw Arjun losing his balance, he spoke to him, 'Do not give way to grief. Born as warriors, we have to live and die by weapons. Warriors have to be always ready to die. When we pick up arms and go out into the battlefield, we are walking with death. Abhimanyu died a warrior's death, a hero's death. You should be proud of him and so should his wife and mother.' Then Krishna further advised, 'If you give way to grief, your brothers and other kings will lose heart. So stop grieving, get up and infuse courage in the hearts of others.'

Arjun calmed down.

He sat down with his soldiers to get the details of the ghastly incident. It seemed that senior Kaurava warriors surrounded Abhimanyu and killed him by attacking him when he had lost all his weapons. Arjun's boundless grief was swiftly replaced by boundless anger. He swore to kill those who killed his son the next day. He had come back to his original warrior self. He had regained his balance. From where did he get it? From within himself. With a bit of help from Krishna of course.

Something similar had happened in the beginning of the war too. Seeing his cousins, other relatives and old friends, Arjun had lost his balance of mind and had refused to fight. At that time too, it was Krishna who helped him understand his duty as a warrior and the importance of the task ahead of him. It was a war against tyranny and injustice. Arjun was duty-bound as a warrior to fight. That lecture of Krishna to Arjun is famously known as the Bhagavad Gita.

Krishna knew Arjun's nature; he knew his propensity for losing his balance. So, he managed to join him in the war as his personal charioteer. But more than his charioteer, Krishna was Arjun's counsellor and guide.

The Pandavas had to win the war of Mahabharata. Arjun had a huge role to play in it. It was important that he did not lose his balance at any point. Krishna's presence with him ensured that.

Krishna constantly reminded Arjun that the balance is

within, and that one should never lose sight of it.

Balance here means a kind of equilibrium, a sense of harmony, a sense of peace. If we are at such a mental state, we do well both at the work and home fronts. It's a circle; we are satisfied at work, it makes us happy at home; we are happy at home, it leads to better work performance, and so on.

In the words of the world's richest man, CEO and president of Amazon, Jeff Bezos, 'If I'm happy at work, I'm better at home—a better husband and a better father. And if I'm happy at home, I come into work more energized—a better employee and a better colleague.'

There are four things that we need to do to achieve this state of mind:

1. Letting go of perfectionism
2. Developing resilience
3. Restructuring life
4. Exercising

Letting go of perfectionism: Perfectionism certainly provides the driving force leading to accomplishment. But, perfectionists also have the tendency to go overboard. They start having unrealistic expectations. They are inflexible to change, which poses a problem in unforeseen circumstances. When they are unable to achieve what they have set out for, the perfectionists snap under the pressure, they slide into depression. Too much of anything is bad, including perfectionism. We need to strive for excellence more than perfection. And we need to retain our flexibility to handle the dynamics of the forever-changing environment, including people.

Developing resilience: This is the natural second step after letting go of perfectionism. Resilient people have better control over their lives than reactive people. Reactive people have less control over their lives and are prone to stress. To a great extent, technological advancement has fanned reactive behaviour in people. We need to know the whereabouts of our subordinates, our children, because it is easy to do so. So we react when we do not get emails, texts or calls from people we are expecting to be in touch with us. We are actually, practically, giving our control to our phones. And it is stressing us out. When we show resilience and not check emails over dinner, we feel better and in control. This habit needs to be worked upon. We need to unplug to retain our balance and sanity in this world full of gadgets that control us while pretending to help.

Restructuring life: Many times, without realizing it, we fall into a rut. That in itself is so stressful. So, from time to time, we need to pause and evaluate our work life as well as our personal life. We need to make a list of all our time-wasting activities and people, and get rid of them. Internet surfing and updating our social media platforms are common time-wasting activities. Then there are always some friends who just want to chill out and do nothing in the evenings. They can be limited to once a week. This is like spring cleaning our life. It gives us a sense of control as well as freedom. Prioritizing our tasks is a good habit for work as well as home. Setting short-term and long-term goals helps to streamline life and avoids confusion and stress.

Exercising: All the machines need to be serviced, and so do our bodies. As we take care of our eating and sleeping habits, so should we look after the exercising of our body. Exercising releases feel-good endorphins in our body, which are natural stress-busters. Twenty minutes of yoga, brisk walk or any exercise is recommended to keep the heart pumping optimally, and the muscles and joints moving smoothly. Deep breathing is recommended for five minutes in the morning to help kick-start the day on an energized yet relaxed note. Considering we are discussing balance, the body also plays a role in it. A tired body cannot have a balanced mind.

Achieving work-life balance is not enough for a leader. They have to instil it in their subordinates as well. After all, if the team members are stressed out or unhappy, how can the leader hope to achieve any sense of peace at work!

There are four things we can do to encourage work-life balance in our subordinates:

1. Create flexible work schedules
2. Honour the subordinate's vacation time
3. Discourage working after office hours
4. Plan quarterly family meets
5. Become a role model

Create flexible work schedules: This can be done while preparing the plan of action for the project. As long as the deliverables are in sight, the work schedules can be chalked out with the entire team participating in the planning process. Flexible time schedules encourage collaborative action and create a stress-free work environment. Individual efficiency increases and the team achieves the target faster.

Honour the subordinate's vacation time: Normally, when some team member is on leave, he or she continues to get calls and emails from the office. How is that fair? If a vacation cannot give us mental and physical relaxation, then it defeats the purpose. There should be a rule in the organization that people on vacation are not to be disturbed, unless there is an emergency. So that, when they return to office, they are refreshed and are rearing to get back to work. If work keeps bothering them all through their vacation, they wouldn't want to return happily, would they?

Discourage working after office hours: We should not encourage workaholism, as its side effects are quick burnout of the person. It is bad for the worker, their family as well as the organization. Working extra hours does not show commitment, as some wrongly believe. In fact, completing the task at hand within the given time frame shows efficiency as well as commitment.

Plan quarterly family meets: Some organizations plan annual holidays where all the team members and their families go together to some exotic destination and have a good time. But, not all the team members may want to or are able to do that due to their own other family commitments. It is better to have quarterly meets where whoever can come with their family can join and unwind. That way, the team members will have a choice not to attend all the meets. Anything that becomes mandatory causes stress. Here also, the individuals should have a choice.

Become a role model: This is the most important thing of all. Subordinates have an unconscious tendency to emulate their leader. If we remain in a state of balance, our team members will also reflect that.

At the end of the day, we need to go to bed happily and enjoy a good sleep. That happens only when we are at peace within. And according to Krishna, the control is in our hands.

7.

Krishna on Rules

Learn the rules to play better than the others.

We are surrounded by different kinds of rules. Soon after we are born, the rules begin—from parents to school, from college to work, rules for driving, crossing the road, playing games, running an organization, running a country—rules are everywhere. They are like the air we breathe.

A rule is an authoritative statement of what to do and what not to do in a particular situation. A competent person or a group of persons issue it. Rules can be unwritten understanding, as the ones at home, or written guidelines for using a gadget, etc. Another kind of rules are written commands and polices, which, if not followed, incur punishment.

Rules are meant to systematize and streamline processes to make our lives easier. But, given in the wrong hands to implement them, they can also cause havoc, because living beings, especially humans, do not take kindly to enforcement and suppression.

I am sure we all remember how we used to hate doing the cursive writing homework of making those curls and swirls in rows and rows forever. It was so limiting, though a good exercise to improve our handwriting. But we loved doing craft projects like making a letterbox or a house, as that gave us some sense of freedom regarding how to do it and with what. These are the little freedoms that one looks for within the rules. This is at a very simplistic level.

When we talk of organizations, and need to follow the organizational rules as well as the law of the land, then we start looking for loopholes. The lawyers make a fortune of leading their clients out through the various loopholes that they manage to discover in the long lists of rules and laws.

Certain fields like those of sports have to be stricter in rule enforcement, as the competition is based on that. Sportspersons tend to get carried away by excitement that may lead to aggression, which needs to be reigned in.

Rules of driving need to be enforced, as otherwise there would be chaos and accidents.

Whatever the field may be, one thing is certain, that if we know the rules well, we not only perform well but also are able to anticipate our opponent's moves.

In an organizational scenario, rules might fail occasionally. There could be some subordinates who unintentionally make slip-ups, while some do so intentionally. Human errors can be forgiven but deliberate violations need our attention.

We need to find out the reason/s behind non-compliance. Are the rules relevant and practical? Is the work environment unpleasant? Are the team members happy? Open communication should be encouraged, so that problems, if any, may come to light early and get resolved quickly. Regular monitoring should also be done to reign in miscreants. If the violator does not mend his ways after receiving a warning, then it's better to let such people go. Nobody is worth causing disturbance in the workflow of an organization.

But there are some rules that need to be changed. One old rule that certainly needs to change is: 'Strive to maintain the balance, but react quickly if any change happens.' This rule should be replaced by: 'Do not wait for change to hit you. Anticipate it, plan for it and make it happen on your terms.'

Only if we understand the rules well can we anticipate what is coming next. Krishna used this strategy all the time and thus was always a step ahead of the opponent or the competitor.

Once Arjun was passing through the city of Prabhas, near Dwarka, when he heard about the beauty of Subhadra, Krishna's sister. And like any other young man, he was keen on meeting her. Arjun approached Krishna seeking a meeting with his sister. Unfortunately, Krishna's elder brother Balaram had already committed Subhadra to Arjun's cousin Duryodhan.

Krishna knew about his brother's fondness for sages and hermits. He suggested that Arjun should disguise himself as a hermit and visit Balaram.

Arjun followed his friend's advice.

On meeting the disguised Arjun, as per the rules of those times, Balaram invited the hermit to stay in their palace complex. He also deputed Subhadra to look after the guest. This was also part of the rules of etiquette.

And this was exactly what Arjun had wanted.

Subhadra looked after Arjun well, but was surprised to note that the hermit behaved more like a prince rather a hermit. She was attracted to him. Meanwhile, Arjun, the hermit, had already fallen in love with Subhadra. He confessed this to Krishna and again asked for his advice.

Krishna first confirmed from Subhadra that she also loved the strange hermit. When he told her about the true identity of the hermit, Subhadra was even more pleased, as she had heard a lot about Arjun's valour. She now desired to marry Arjun rather than his conceited cousin Duryodhan.

Considering that Balaram had given his word to Duryodhan, the situation became awkward. As a rule, a warrior could not break his promise. Balaram was bound by his promise to Duryodhan. How could Krishna tell his brother to break his word!

But Krishna had a plan. He knew how to skirt around the rules.

A festival was to be held at the Raivataka Hill. Subhadra would be there with her friends. Krishna suggested to Arjun that he should go to that festival and abduct his ladylove. He even gave his chariot to him for a swift getaway. It was not a suggestion one would expect from Krishna. But then, he knew that the only way to get Arjun and Subhadra together would be for them to run away together.

Arjun followed his friend's advice. Shedding his disguise, he dressed up like the prince that he was, and rode to Raivataka in Krishna's chariot. Soon enough, he spotted his ladylove. Arjun spurred the horses and rushed towards Subhadra. In no time, he had taken hold of her hand and pulled her into his chariot. And before anyone could react,

Arjun had sped away. It was a daring daylight kidnapping indeed!

Naturally, Balaram and the entire Yadava clan, except Krishna, were upset. Seeing the Pandava Prince Arjun's audacity, the Yadavas decided to wage a war on the Pandavas. According to them, Arjun could have approached Balaram for Subhadra's hand, like any other suitor, instead of abducting the girl. This was a gross insult to Balaram as well as Subhadra, they felt.

Krishna did not agree. According to him, no rules were broken. Arjun behaved like a hero, abducting the woman he loved. This was acceptable behaviour from a great warrior like him. He further suggested that an alliance with the powerful Pandavas would help the Yadavas, whereas fighting and losing would bring them disgrace, since no man on earth was capable of vanquishing Arjun in battle.

Krishna then reminded Balaram that Arjun belonged to the illustrious Bharata clan and his mother Kunti was their father Vasudeva's sister, belonging to the Yadava clan. So, in all respects, Arjun was a great match for their sister Subhadra.

Satisfied that no rules were broken, Balaram accepted his younger brother's arguments gracefully. Emissaries were sent to the Pandavas, with gifts, to bring back Arjun and Subhadra. The city of Dwarka was decked up and a proper wedding took place with much festivity.

Everything worked out as planned by Krishna.

Ilsa J. Bick, an award-winning author, says, 'Sticking to rules just because they are there does not make them right. You need to learn when the rules should be broken.'

Essentially, we need to understand the rules so well

that we should be able to find ways around them. This understanding also helps in abandoning old rules and formulating new ones.

There are seven golden rules for making rules:

1. Start with the most important rule
2. Refer to organizations having a similar line of work
3. Don't be too harsh
4. Don't be too soft
5. Include a clause for forgiveness
6. Be available
7. Be adaptable

Start with the most important rule: This is common sense. People start losing interest as they go on reading.

Refer to organizations having a similar line of work: It certainly helps to know what other organizations are giving and what people expect. We should not repeat the mistakes that others are doing, and for that we ought to know how organizations similar to ours function—how do they retain their workforce, their vendors and their clients.

Don't be too harsh: It is important not to be dictatorial. Not everyone can function their best under pressure. People should be allowed to express their grievances.

Don't be too soft: If the rules are not enforced and people are allowed to get away with breaking them, it would result in chaos. The productivity of the organization will go down drastically. Rules and discipline help to streamline an organization.

Include a clause for forgiveness: This is very important. Those who have broken any rule unintentionally need not always be punished. Giving a stern warning and letting them off often helps.

Be available: Sometimes the team members may give useful ideas, so we must be available with a listening ear. It also helps to instil confidence and a sense of security in the subordinates.

Be adaptable: It is important to think ahead at all times. The bigger picture should be understood. The challenges that could come in the future should be anticipated and planned for. We should be ready to plan ahead and adapt to changes that seem inevitable. And for that, an out-of-the-box approach may be required; if the rules need to be modified or changed altogether, so be it.

Arjun's falling in love with Subhadra was a challenge that came Krishna's way. He could not make his brother break his promise to Duryodhan, as warriors were quite strict about the rules governing their lives—making a promise to someone was one of the toughest rules to break.

Krishna used the rule of welcoming a hermit to the royal palace and offering hospitality to him till whenever he wanted to stay. This rule enabled Arjun to get close to Subhadra, incognito.

The time of Duryodhan's arrival for his impending wedding with Subhadra was drawing near. It was yet another challenge for Krishna to handle. He had to think out of the box. The idea of Arjun abducting Subhadra in front of everyone was a daring act and required a revisiting of rules.

In the case of organizations, the rules, if carefully selected and fairly enforced, help in the smooth running and effective management of the workforce. The rules also protect the organization from litigation and other such issues. Apart from the required rules and policies, there are many other optional rules that must also be looked into. These can vary for different organizations.

1. Safety rules related to the workplace and gadgets or machines that are being used
2. Policy for leaves of absence
3. Policy for overtime
4. Policy for recording the work hours
5. Policy for lunch and tea breaks
6. Dress code
7. Rules for using the employer's property
8. Policy regarding workplace violence
9. Policy regarding hiring people with a criminal history

The above rules are basic but very important for the smooth running of any organization. They help create discipline in the workplace, which in turn enhances the efficiency of the team members. Because of the basic nature of these rules, there is normally no opposition to them.

Certain owners may want more specific rules added to the list above—rules related to the political and off-duty activities of the team members, working freelance after office hours, and so on. Such rules are mostly negotiable.

Four cardinal points should be considered while selecting or formulating work rules to ensure a pleasant work atmosphere for the team, resulting in enhanced productivity. They are:

1. Creating an atmosphere where the team members are treated with respect
2. Helping to ensure that the team members conduct themselves professionally
3. Encouraging communication with the management
4. Ensuring that all team members are treated fairly

In case we feel the need to create a new rule, the following checklist should be kept in mind:

1. Is this rule really necessary?
2. How will this rule impact the team members?
3. What extra documentation would be required to implement this rule?
4. What would be the consequence of non-compliance?
5. Is there a precedent for this sort of rule?

Pablo Picasso, the great artist, once said, 'Learn the rules like a pro, so you can break them like an artist.' And then make new ones!

The bottom line remains: Learn the rules well to play better.

8.

Krishna on Stability

Emotional stability is the key to success.

My favourite definition of stability is 'the strength to endure'. And emotional stability is the capacity to withstand difficult situations, handle adversity and remain productive throughout. It is the boxing equivalent to being able to take a punch, stay grounded and not panic.

In any organization, more than one's intelligence quotient, one's emotional quotient and emotional stability play larger roles in ensuring success. Emotions can be motivating as well as debilitating. Successful leaders utilize their emotional intelligence to manage their own emotions, as well as those of others.

Then there are those leaders who lack emotional intelligence and end up losing their own emotional balance, and subsequently that of their team. Unconsciously, such people use certain words that may seem innocuous but turn out to be lethal for the listener's mental and emotional health.

This is very commonly seen in a family scenario. The parents reprimand the child for not getting good grades, and while scolding they tell their child how stupid or lazy he or she has been. This approach does not necessarily fetch good grades in the future. In fact, it demotivates the child.

The choice of words used by a leader shows his own state of mental and emotional stability. The wrong words can push the team towards instability.

Certain adjectives should be avoided when describing or addressing a team member:

1. *Dumb:* This is a very misused adjective. It should never be used in a workplace scenario. It undermines a person completely and is a big blow to his or her self-confidence.
2. *Fool:* Like dumb, this is also a strongly negative adjective. It also undermines a person and kills their self-confidence.
3. *Irresponsible:* This is a strong word and should be used only where absolutely necessary.
4. *Incompetent:* This is a favourite with the bosses. They use it to reprimand the subordinates. But every time a person hears that he or she is incompetent, their self-esteem takes a dip. It gets depressing and might result in that person quitting the job.
5. *Disappointment:* There is nothing worse than being told that you are a disappointment. The better way is to express disappointment in the action rather than the person.
6. *Lazy:* This also hurts as it implies absence of drive in a person, whereas the drive could just be lesser than usual, and that too for some not-so-apparent reason.
7. *Weird:* This is a judgmental word and best used among friends. It has no place in the office environment.

8. *Mad:* Calling someone mad is downright rude. Again, this word can be used among friends where things are taken light-heartedly. In an office scenario, it should be deleted from our vocabulary.

Things do not always go the way we want them to. At that moment we get angry or upset or frustrated with everything and everyone around us. That is a testing moment for us actually. We need to keep our language in check and not use negative words, because our anger is momentary and would dissipate but the words that we throw around would linger on in the environment and get lodged in the psyche of the team members.

Some such negative words are:

1. *Failure:* This word should be left outside the organization. The very thought of failure should be shunned. Success should be the word of choice.
2. *Can't:* If a person trusts us and we tell them that they can't do a particular thing, they would actually believe it. And this is not fair to them, because then they would not even try to do it, as they would be convinced of their incapability.
3. *Ashamed:* This is a very heartbreaking word and pushes the person into the abyss of embarrassment. It should be used very sparingly, if at all.
4. *Hate:* This word reeks of racism and should never be used in a workplace. It hurts deeply and seeds discrimination. Such emotions spread swiftly and can spoil the environment of the entire organization.
5. *Wrong:* This is a strong word and best used only when

we are sure that the situation demands it. It should not be used casually as it can leave a bad feeling in the person for whom it's used.

Aristotle, the Greek philosopher-scientist, has summed it up well: 'Getting angry is okay so long as you get angry for the right reason with the right person to the right degree using the right words with the right tone of voice and appropriate language.' Aristotle, the Greek philosopher-scientist, has summed it up well.

If we observe Krishna's life, we would find that he never lost his cool. He faced a number of demons, ogres, evil kings and other enemies all through his life, as that was his job—to vanquish them. But, he faced every situation with equanimity and came out a winner. And that is exactly what he kept advising his friends and family too.

In the battle of Mahabharata, when the stalwarts began to be killed, emotions were running very high on both the sides. On the evening of the 14th day of the battle, the rule of ceasefire at sunset was not followed. As the passions rose, the restraints broke down. The fight continued through the night with torchlights.

Ghatotkach was the son of Pandava Bheem and his wife, demoness Hidimbi. He was a giant demon endowed with magical powers. It is well known that the demons are at their powerful best in the darkness of the night. So, considering that the war was continuing beyond the scheduled time, Krishna sent Ghatotkach to attack Karna that night.

Ghatotkach and his troops, empowered by the darkness, went about annihilating the Kaurava army in thousands, using their magical powers.

Ghatotkach himself attacked Karna. Duryodhan, the eldest Kaurava, could not stand this anymore and ordered his friend Karna to kill Ghatotkach immediately.

Karna had a celestial missile gifted to him by Lord Indra. He had saved it to kill Arjun, his archenemy. He was himself a formidable warrior, one of the most powerful ones in the world, but so was Arjun. Karna didn't want to take any chances and so kept the celestial weapon as a standby. He could not waste it on anyone else.

Karna fought valiantly for a long time but the darkness-powered demons were getting to him too. Duryodhan was also putting a lot of pressure on him to kill the leader of the demons, Ghatotkach. Feeling cornered, Karna decided to use his celestial weapon, though grudgingly. The unfortunate thing about this missile was that it could kill only one person and then would self-destruct.

Finally, Karna shot the celestial missile at Ghatotkach, who, on seeing it coming, expanded his size phenomenally. The missile killed him instantly and he fell on the Kaurava army, killing thousands under him.

Ghatotkach's death plunged the Pandava camp into gloom. Bheem was inconsolable. Only Krishna seemed pleased. Why?

Arjun was understandably upset at Krishna's lack of empathy. It was Krishna who had urged Ghatotkach to fight with Karna. Now that he was dead, and Karna was still alive, the least Krishna could do was to offer his condolences to the bereaved father Bheem. But instead, he was looking unusually happy.

On being confronted by Arjun, Krishna admitted that he

was pleased with the turn of the events. He explained why:

'I am happy that Karna used his celestial missile on Ghatotkach. It was a one-time weapon. No person on this earth could have survived that missile, not even you, Arjun. My own Sudarshan Chakra also couldn't have stopped it. Ghatotkach had to die, but with him died the missile. Yes, Bheem's son is dead, but then so is yours and so are other sons. This is a war and the warriors are doing their jobs. And they are doing it well. Ghatotkach killed lakhs of Kaurava soldiers before he died.'

Arjun saw the truth in Krishna's words.

'Without his celestial missile, Karna has now become vulnerable. It would be easy for you, dear Arjun, to kill him. The end of the Kauravas is drawing near. Victory will soon be yours. This thought is making me happy,' Krishna explained the logic to Arjun.

Situations like these would continue to come in our lives, where we would be overwhelmed by emotions. We are not to allow those emotions to ride us. We need to over-ride our emotions and remain calm. Only then can we think sensibly and take the next step forward.

Arjun saw the truth in Krishna's words. Since they were warriors, their first duty was to the job at hand, which was fighting unto death to win the war. Ghatotkach was like any other warrior; he died for a cause. That day was over; they had to plan for the next day.

Krishna explained that the real stability in a person's character comes from his emotional stability. And that stability helps him to tackle any crisis and makes him successful in every field.

Analysing the above incident, we come to three basic factors that help us maintain emotional stability in any given situation:

1. Adjusting perspective
2. Reworking expectations
3. Moving on

Adjusting perspective: Every situation has at least two perspectives, if not more. We tend to adopt the worst one. It is normal, because negative events are likely to create negative thoughts and biases. The trick here is to pause and look at the event from the other side. There is always something positive hidden behind it. Every cloud has a silver lining, as they say. The moment we change our perspective, we realize that the event is not as bad as we thought it to be.

Ghatotkach's death was bad, but hidden behind it was the fact that Karna had lost the deadly weapon that was meant to kill Arjun. So, in reality, losing Ghatotkach saved Arjun. Ghatotkach wouldn't have won the war for the Pandavas but Arjun would, and did.

Reworking expectations: The root cause of any emotional disturbance is the unfulfilled expectation behind it. We do not ever expect bad things to happen to us. And when they do, we get emotionally disturbed. The moment we think rationally, we would realize that bad things can happen to anyone, including us. That understanding helps to handle the shock of any untoward incident better.

Ghatotkach was not immortal. He fought bravely and died, like many before and many after him. When a warrior goes to war, he may or may not return—we cannot expect him to come back safe and sound, we can only wish it.

Moving on: This is the most important step in regaining emotional stability. Whatever happened has happened and cannot be undone. Pondering over it and justifying it contribute towards inaction, which is counterproductive. The best way out is to get back into action mode and create a plan for the next step forward.

After Ghatotkach's death, the next step forward for the Pandavas was to attack Karna.

The rules of work have changed. It is not just a person's qualifications or experience that matter now. Organizations want more. They want to know how well we handle ourselves under stress and how well we handle other team members. Emotional intelligence is the most sought-after soft skill in today's corporate world.

What does it entail?

Emotional intelligence or emotional stability does not necessarily mean that we have to be nice to everyone at all times. In fact, confronting people with facts that they have been avoiding to acknowledge may be the need of the hour at times. But then, it also does not mean giving a free reign to our feelings and reactions. Rather, it means managing our feelings in a way as to express them in the right measure to effectively enable people to work smoothly towards the common target.

Dr Tomas Chamorro-Premuzic, an organizational psychologist working in the area of leadership development, says, 'A good manager is an even-tempered people person who has the skills to delegate technical tasks, give feedback and foster trust and emotional stability.'

Many times we find ourselves multitasking and working long hours. The resultant fatigue may cause emotional instability. The ups and downs of our personal life may also occupy our mind and cause imbalance. There could be other factors like lack of job satisfaction, attitudinal differences with colleagues, adjustment issues in the city and so on. All these stresses are 'normal' in the sense that we all go through them.

The first step then, on the road to becoming a good leader, is to learn how to de-stress. Taking breaks to get away from work as well as the city is quite therapeutic. Talking to the boss to clarify confusions if any, and making friends with colleagues, also helps to dilute work-related stresses.

Once we learn to manage our personal stresses, we become better equipped to handle the larger issues at our workplace. We would then be able to maintain our emotional balance and lead our team to success.

At the end of the day, we must realize that to be successful in life, we need to be emotionally stable, and to maintain that equanimity, we need to change our perspectives, be realistic in our expectations and learn to move on.

9.

Krishna on Behaviour

Behaviour speaks louder than words.

Behaviour is defined as the way we act or conduct ourselves, especially towards others.

It is a well-known fact that learning happens by imitation. Every parent has seen that whatever moral values or etiquette they may try to teach their children, the actual learning happens from what they see around themselves. It is impossible to teach them not to hit anyone by using corporal punishment. Hence the idiom, 'Practice what you preach'.

Meg Wheatley, an American management consultant who studies organizational behaviour, says, 'Leadership is a series of behaviours rather than a role for heroes.'

John Quincy Adams, the sixth US President reiterates, 'If your actions inspire the others to dream more, learn more, do more and become more, you are a leader.'

But then nobody is perfect. Everyone makes mistakes.

We can be assured that the leadership has issues when we see an organization's performance dropping below optimal level. On careful observation, we will notice that the CEO is doing the following:

1. *Behaving like a dictator:* It is not the right of the

leader to order people around, as many tend to think. When that happens, good team members leave. The ones who are left behind due to some compulsions, work grudgingly under such a leader. When no one is happy, the results can't be good.

2. *Neglecting clients:* Many leaders get so wrapped up in their own label or designation that they forget the jurisdiction of the label. After all, they head only their own team or organization, and not anyone else outside of it. These leaders get so carried away that they end up neglecting their clients or customers. Considering that any organization exists only for its customers, such behaviour certainly affects the health of the organization.

3. *Believing themselves to be superior to all*: People tend to forget that being a leader is a privilege and not a permanent crown on the head. They are not special or superior from the rest of the team. Also it's worth remembering that the leader also has a boss—the owner of the organization—who can hire and fire as well. 'Nobody is indispensable' holds true for the team leader, too.

4. *Humiliating subordinates in public*: This is probably the worst behaviour a leader can exhibit. It almost always leads to the path of self-destruction. The subordinates start objecting and then rebelling against their leader. The productivity of the organization goes down the drain. Finally, the leader has to be replaced by a better person to help the organization recover.

5. *Surrounding themselves with yes-men*: People, who

constantly need validation or ego pampering are bad choice for leading. They indulge in blatant favouritism and as a result, start losing respect from the rest of the team. Such leaders cannot think beyond themselves; they are unable to handle dissent. Under such a leadership, the organization would stagnate and eventually decline.

6. *Threatening subordinates and vendors*: Threats never work. They actually reveal the inherent insecurities of the person who is threatening. It drives people away. The vendors would go to another buyer. The subordinates would either rebel or quit. Either way, the performance of the team and the organization drops.

American motivational speaker Jim Rohn has summed it up quite neatly, 'The challenge of leadership is to be strong, but not rude; be kind, but not weak; be bold, but not a bully; be humble, but not timid; be proud, but not arrogant; have humour, but without folly.'

A leader's role is crucial in a crisis. Any war is a culmination of a crisis. The great war of Mahabharata was no different. It lasted 18 days and resulted in the destruction of the Kauravas.

The Pandavas were victorious, but the eldest of the Pandava brothers, Yudhishthir, was not happy. In fact, he was stricken with remorse. The war had killed his cousins, his teachers and so many other relatives. While performing the last rites of his relatives, Yudhishthir went into depression and refused to take over the throne of Hastinapur. He wanted to give up everything and go to the forests instead, to lead the life of a hermit.

Arjun was irritated by his brother's attitude of not appreciating how tough it was to win the war. He disagreed with him and so did the other Pandava brothers and their wife Draupadi. Sages Vyasa and Narada also tried to persuade Yudhishthir to change his mind, but in vain.

It was Krishna who managed to convince Yudhishthir to enjoy his victory.

He explained to Yudhishthir his duties as a king, the first being to behave like one. He was the eldest of the Kuru clan now and the rightful heir to the throne. He had a responsibility, not only towards his family, but also towards the people of Hastinapur. If he had to kill his cousins, it was only because they were evildoers and had to be brought to justice. He was only performing his duty as a warrior and the king of Indraprastha, the estate his cousins had wrested away from him deceitfully.

Yudhishthir entered Hastinapur and was crowned as King by Krishna.

Krishna did not leave things here. He went a step ahead and took Yudhishthir to meet the dying Bheeshma. Why? Because, all his life Bheeshma was the de facto ruler of Hastinapur, though he never sat on the throne himself. First his stepbrother, then his nephew and then his nephew's son— while they became kings, Bheeshma stood behind them as their guide. He was the best person to guide Yudhishthir too, as the latter was also incidentally Bheeshma's grandnephew.

Thus, Bheeshma gave a long discourse to Yudhishthir on how to rule wisely and justly. He lectured Yudhishthir on the importance of leadership behaviour, on how to behave like a king—a king commands respect by his behaviour and not by demanding it. Actions always speak louder than words.

The leadership behaviours that are seen in all the great leaders are:

1. They teach
2. They listen
3. They love challenges
4. They carve their own path
5. They inspire
6. They don't complain

Good leaders teach: Apple CEO Tim Cook credits the company's success to Steve Jobs's role as a teacher. According to him, the reason why the company continues to grow in size and value is because Steve Jobs taught his team what matters most, so they could teach their own teams, and so on.

Krishna taught Arjun, and he taught Yudhishthir as well. He also took Yudhishthir to one of the greatest leaders of his time, and one of the greatest teachers too—Bheeshma.

Good leaders listen: Listening means appreciating others, and it is the best way to build trust. It also helps to foresee problems before they happen. Listening leads to well-thought-out decisions. A successful leader is always open to new and different perspectives. Someone once rightly said, courage is not just standing up to speak; it is also sitting down to listen.

Good leaders love challenges: They do not pat themselves on the back for a job well done, or a landmark achievement. Good leaders praise their team for the success and immediately move on to the next challenge.

Good leaders carve their own path: Successful leaders learn from their own experiences. They may serve and learn from their mentors, but they do not become followers. They carve their own path. They trust their own intuition. They create their own way of doing things. They are innovative themselves and encourage innovation in their subordinates.

Good leaders inspire: They have a vision for the future, which they express with much passion and energy. This motivates and inspires their subordinates and fires them into action. Successful leaders infuse their teams with their own strong beliefs and values. Leaders are those who others follow. Great leaders are driven by their own vision, their obsession, and they are focussed on making it happen. This quality inspires others to follow.

Good leaders don't complain: Most leaders have risen from the ranks; they have faced and overcome adversity. They do not believe in complaining about problems; they believe in resolving the problems.

As can be seen, leaders are defined by their behaviour, what they do or don't do, how they act or don't act. Being a leader means huge responsibility, as their followers imitate them. A leader who behaves like a monster would create an army of monsters.

This was also evident in the Mahabharata. The Kaurava brothers were led by their eldest brother, the evil Duryodhan. He hated his cousins, the Pandavas, and was always planning ways to destroy them. He managed to convince his father, brothers, uncles and other relatives that the Pandavas were no good. Ultimately, a small feud turned into a big war, destroying Duryodhan himself along with his brothers.

Not everyone is born a leader; effective leadership skills can be cultivated with time and patience. Strong leaders can transform an organization's work culture from top to bottom, and drive the team members to follow their mission forward, while engaging with the present realities and keeping an eye on the future at the same time.

Let us see what all key leadership practices are required for becoming an effective leader.

1. Adopting a democratic approach
2. Charting a path
3. Seeking critical feedback

Adopting a democratic approach: An effective leader makes all his subordinates feel that they have something to offer. And many times, the best of solutions can come from the lowest of people in the corporate hierarchy. So, it is important to make everyone feel like a part of the organization, like one big family. This behaviour creates good bonding among the team members, and working cohesively increases the efficiency and productivity of the organization.

Charting a path: The progress of an organization depends on the path towards its goal. A clearly defined goal and an equally planned out path gives succinct direction to the team members. An effective leader charts out a path for his team, with regular checkpoints to monitor their progress. He clarifies the key outcomes desired and the principle strategies agreed upon to reach those outcomes. People following a path are more likely to achieve their target rather than those sprinting straight to the deadline. A true leader not only leads, but also guides. He has to behave like a parent at times, showing the way by torchlight. And when a team member trips on the path, the leader holds his hand to make him cross the hurdle.

Seeking critical feedback: Feedback is an important part of management. Everyone appreciates a good feedback, but an effective leader looks forward to even a negative feedback. He uses that opportunity to rectify his mistakes. Then he goes a step further and shares with his subordinates how not to commit the mistake that he did. Great leaders know that critical feedback helps them to learn and grow. They are not afraid to share their mistakes, so their team performs better. Sharing is caring holds true here too—sharing the lesson learnt, in this case.

Ownership does not necessarily mean leadership. In the anecdote from Krishna's life, it is clearly seen that though the kingdom of Hastinapur belonged to Yudhishthir, he was not behaving like a leader, like the king that he was. Krishna had to shake him out of his stupor to make him understand the meaning of leadership and the responsibilities that go with it. Krishna had to teach Yudhishthir how to behave like a leader.

Human behaviour flows from three main sources: desire, emotion and knowledge. Out of these, knowledge is acquired all the time and it helps us to reach rational decisions. Desires and emotions are labile. Mostly, it is seen that desires lead to emotions.

Yudhishthir's reason for backing off from taking the responsibility of ruling over his kingdom was his perceived guilt. Krishna told him in no uncertain terms that his fight was not yet over. He still had to fight his mental demons of desires and emotions.

Krishna explained to Yudhishthir that in order to maintain his mental balance, he would have to banish his emotion of sorrow. He had to be objective and in control of his desires and emotions. Only then could he rule effectively. An emotionally distraught leader can never lead his people.

The leader has to, first and foremost, be in control of himself, before thinking of controlling people and running an organization. He has to behave the way he wants his team members to behave. It is an ancient saying: We change other people's behaviour by changing our own.

Once we keep our desires and emotions in check, the knowledge that we have guides our behaviour.

And as Krishna says, 'Example is leadership.'

10.

Krishna on Decision-Making

Do not let your emotions make your decisions.

Decision-making is a daily activity for all of us. Right from childhood we are taught and are expected to make our own decisions—decisions that are useful on a long-term basis. Choosing subjects to study further is one such example where the decision has a long-term target of acquiring a sustainable career. Buying a flat is another example where the decision affects all the inmates of that flat.

In an organization, decision-making is a crucial process, where success or failure of the decisions made result in profits or losses for the organization. A bad choice of an employee could result in losses of man-hours, which affects the growth of the organization. A joint venture with a weak partner can result in huge financial losses. In fact, every aspect of running an organization involves critical decision-making.

The decision maker is not only responsible for the growth of his organization but also the sustenance of that growth. And that is the cause of intense stress for most in such positions. Till the time the decisions are empirical, they are easier to take, but when any emotion creeps in, the situation becomes tricky.

This happens a lot.

Many times the decision maker is not even aware how he got tricked into making a wrong decision. These days, not only friends and family, but social media also feeds us with emotional triggers. A piece of fake news or wrong statistics on Twitter of Facebook can cause havoc in related decisions.

Anxiety about something unrelated to work, like spouse's health or loan repayment for a new flat, can result in clouding our judgment and our decision-making capacity. Likewise, intense happiness or sadness about unrelated achievement or loss can also cloud our decision-making. When we are excited or happy, we tend to underestimate the risk factors. Similarly, sadness makes us set the bar low.

Intense emotions lead to rash decisions. Anger and embarrassment make us vulnerable to high-risk, low-payoff choices. This is a scourge of modern times. Leading lives on a fast lane has its pitfalls, and getting trapped in emotionally coloured decisions is one of them.

Let us take a leaf out of Krishna's life to see how he can help us get over this problem.

Krishna was always a very reasonable person, even as a child. He did not indulge in anything out of sheer emotion. His naughtiness was a part of his charm. His pranks were always innocent and more like a show of affection, rather than something done out of malice.

When he did not listen to his mother and went across the river to play with his friends, it was not that he wanted to disobey his parents or was rebelling in some way. He went because he wanted to rid the place of a nasty demon.

Krishna's life is full of such incidents, but those were part of his job, so to speak. After all, he had come to rid the world of evil, like the other incarnations of Vishnu.

Coming back to the point of emotions, one of Krishna's main teachings was that we must control our emotions and not allow them to rule us. He maintained that emotions are not bad but ought to be harnessed as energies and used constructively. Otherwise, when emotions are allowed to take control, they end up in destruction. Essentially, he advocated the wise use of emotions.

As a youngster, once Krishna saw his entire village preparing for some event, a huge sacrifice of sorts. It was an annual event in their village, but had gone unnoticed by Krishna, maybe because he was too young to ponder over it earlier. Anyway, this time Krishna asked his foster father Nanda about it.

'For whom are you—in fact, everyone—doing this sacrifice? What would it accomplish? Also, is this sacrifice prescribed in the scriptures? It seems that everyone is involved in it, and when so many people are doing the same thing, it could be that they know what they are doing. But it may also be that they don't; they are just following others.'

It was a very reasonable question and line of thought, considering that everyone in the village was involved in it. It is true that many times, people just do things because they see others doing it; it's a mechanical process for them. But then, even if the majority were doing it mechanically, what about the handful who were doing it in their full senses? The question remains: Why were they doing it?

Krishna mentioned scriptures here because many people perform rituals without bothering to know the reason behind them. If his father had said that the scriptures were being followed, Krishna would certainly have then questioned the knowers of scriptures, the brahmins, about the same.

Nanda explained, 'Lord Indra is the god of rain; the clouds belong to him. Rain, like milk, provides sustenance to all living beings. So, in order to show our gratitude for the rain that comes to us from Indra's clouds, we worship him. This sacrifice is a form of thanksgiving to Lord Indra.'

The other elders also joined in with Nanda to elaborate the importance of sacrifice to Indra. They said that it was an age-old tradition, which if not followed, was sure to bring ruin to the community, by way of famine, etc. After all, if the god of rain was angry, the first thing he would do, would be to remove the clouds from the sky. There would be no rain. How would the crops be sustained? How would the rivers and wells be filled? With no water, how would life be sustained? There would be hunger, sadness and death all around. It was a grim picture indeed.

Krishna was not convinced. He knew his science, the water cycle, the laws of nature, the works. He immediately reacted, 'Our happiness and sadness depend on our own karma and not the anger or appeasement of Indra. We take birth or die due to the force of our own karma. We make our own destiny. The doer is the only controller. Indra cannot alter any living being's destiny.'

Obviously, Indra must not have been pleased to hear this from a mere mortal.

Krishna was not finished yet. He said, 'It is wrong to waste so much money and food by putting them into the fire, just to please a god. All this can be put to better use. Instead of putting the raw cereals, ghee, honey, milk, fruits, etc. into the sacrificial fire, you can cook the food and feed the children and the elderly, the people who help you, the cows who give you milk—feed those who would appreciate it. Why should you waste all this good food just to feed a god's ego?'

Indra had still not lost hope, as after all, the age-old customs cannot be abandoned by the words of one person in a day, or so he thought.

But more and more people had gathered around Nanda and Krishna. The conversation seemed intriguing. The boy was making sense.

'The sun shines every day and the water evaporates from the rivers and lakes and forms clouds. After some time, the clouds become heavy and return the water to the earth as rain. What has Indra got to do with it? This is the cycle of nature. If at all, we should worship nature, we should worship this mountain of ours that gives us so many kinds of fruits, vegetables and grains; we should worship our cows.'

Krishna was very clear that we should not waste our resources on those who do nothing for us. Understanding the value of our resources is very important, as is understanding who is helpful for us. Gratitude should not be misplaced; it should be given where it is due.

Nanda and the rest of the people realized the merit of Krishna's words. They stopped their preparations for the annual sacrifice for Indra, and instead, they celebrated nature, and each other. They worshipped their cows and their mountain, Govardhan, and fed their teachers, the brahmins.

On seeing this, Indra lost his cool. The anger that was seething within him came to the fore. For centuries, he was enjoying the power he felt when the mortals worshipped him before the onset of monsoons. Suddenly, not one person or one family, but the entire village was ignoring him. He was not going to tolerate this rejection, this insult.

The next thing the happy revelling villagers saw was the untimely arrival of monsoon. Suddenly, the sky darkened, wind howled, thunder roared and rain lashed. People ran helter-skelter. The celebrations were washed away and the children started crying in fear. Such a downpour was never seen before by anyone in the village.

As expected, the murmurs started that it was the wrath of Lord Indra. People started regretting listening to Krishna. As the volume of rain swelled, so did the murmurs, till they reached Krishna's ears.

Krishna knew the reason behind this sudden deluge. Obviously, it was Indra's anger. But then, that anger was not right; it was misplaced. That anger came from ego, not injustice. It was Indra's emotional reaction to the action that he didn't like. The action was not wrong, the reaction was.

Krishna did not want the villagers to be scared of Indra and start the practice of sacrifice again. The purpose of the entire exercise would be defeated. So he decided to use his cosmic powers to teach Indra a lesson and show the villagers that they were right in stopping the practice of unnecessary sacrifice.

Krishna came out of his house and with his cosmic powers, lifted the Govardhan Mountain on his left hand. He then called out to his father and others, asking them to take shelter under the mountain. Slowly, the entire village with its cattle was sheltering under the huge mountain, held aloft by Krishna.

Krishna held the mountain up for seven days without

moving from his place. Finally, Indra realized who he was up against. Bereft of his pride and broken in his determination, he left the villagers in peace.

Once the sky was clear and the waters subsided, Krishna asked the villagers to go back to their homes, promising never to be sacred of Indra. Then he gently placed Govardhan Mountain back in its place.

The villagers understood, and since that time started worshipping Govardhan Mountain rather than Indra. They stopped wasting food and started feeding the needy instead.

This is one of many such stories about Krishna's life. At any point of time in his life, however emotionally critical or critically emotional the situation might be, Krishna did not allow his emotions to rule his head.

During the battle of Mahabharata, Krishna taught the same thing to Arjun too. Arjun was getting emotional about killing his relatives and teachers. Krishna taught him to harness his emotions to fight for justice. People always get killed in wars as collateral damage, but that doesn't stop the fight for justice.

Whether in life situations or in work, we need to keep our heads on top of our emotions.

Dale Carnegie once said, 'When dealing with people, remember you are not dealing with creatures of logic, but with creatures of emotion.'

According to a report by World Economic Forum, emotional intelligence is one of the fastest growing job skills, surpassing even technical ability in some cases.

Seeing how Indra got steered by his anger into unleasing havoc on earth, we can understand why intelligent handling of emotions is crucial for effective leadership.

There are four basic emotions that we deal with most of the time in the corporate decision-making scenario:

1. Anger
2. Happiness
3. Sadness
4. Anxiety

Anger: Anger instils confidence, many times bordering on overconfidence or rashness. It makes us eager to take a decision. Anger activates us. It makes us take more risks, which might otherwise be unnecessary. Anger makes us vulnerable to high-risk, low-payoff choices. Angry people tend to blame others easily. It also makes them rely more on stereotypes.

Happiness: Happiness is no better. It makes us too complacent and generous. It makes us ignore the possibility of wrong results. It also makes us underestimate the risks involved in a decision. Happy people want to continue their emotional state and take decisions based on appearances rather than quality or depth.

Sadness: Interestingly, a little sadness may be helpful in weighing pros and cons, though too much sadness won't let us make any decisions at all. Sadness makes us lower the bar and set easier goals. Sad people tend to accept whatever comes their way. They have low expectations for themselves.

Anxiety: Anxiety lingers. If we are anxious about something in our personal life, it will cause us to feel anxious about our business decisions as well. Even if the anxiety-causing situations are different, anxious people are unable to separate them. Anxiety makes people averse to creating or accepting changes.

Hence, in a corporate scenario, it is wise to accept that we are bound to have emotions, but they should not be allowed to influence our decision-making.

A leader, who cannot manage his or her emotions well, can seriously damage employee morale, their performance and eventually the performance and overall success of the company. Hence, managing our emotions effectively at the workplace stands to be a major component of success for us.

How does effective control of emotions help in achieving the desired goals?

There are five ways in which emotional management helps pave the path of success for us:

1. Management of stress levels
2. Development of people skills
3. Graceful acceptance of feedback
4. Setting example
5. Thoughtful decision-making

Management of stress levels: Any and every organization has its own set of workplace pressures. Dealing with these pressures alone is not enough. We also need to function well and to our optimal capacity. Effective control of emotions and subsequent emotional reactions helps us to manage our stress levels effectively.

Development of people skills: Teamwork is important in any workplace. Building relationships with a diverse group of people requires understanding and patience. This is directly related to an effective control of emotions. An ability to listen patiently and respond appropriately to others is a crucial part of people skills. People in control of their emotions are able to set their own emotions aside to lend an ear to someone else. Effective leaders use their emotions to connect with their subordinates to enhance their relationships. They know what to express and how much to let out in a given situation.

Graceful acceptance of feedback: Any feedback is important to the growth of an organization. People in control of their emotions are less defensive and are more open to feedback. They do not take feedback personally, but rather look at it as a means for improvement. The skill of effective, attentive listening also comes in handy here.

Setting example: People who are in control of their emotions, do not get flustered easily when things don't work out as planned. Their knack of getting along with others makes it more likely that people would emulate them. After all, an ability to rise above daily stresses is worth respecting and emulating.

Thoughtful decision-making: All the above points cumulatively lead to thoughtful decision-making. An understanding of people helps the leader to see things from their perspective. This automatically leads to a better judgment of the impact of his or her decision on others.

Effective leaders are acutely aware of their own feelings, but at the same time, they know their responsibility towards their staff, their clients and vendors, and their organization. They have worked on themselves to develop their abilities of keeping their emotions in check when necessary and showing them when the situation calls for it. They have developed the Krishna principle in themselves.

Krishna's handling of Mount Govardhan teaches us that decision-making comprises of four important steps:

1. Identifying the goal
2. Gathering relevant information
3. Evaluating options
4. Making a decision

Identifying the goal: Identifying the goal is the crucial first step, as we need to analyse and understand the problem thoroughly. We need to know what exactly is the problem; why it should be solved; who are the affected parties and if there is any specific deadline or timeline to be followed.

Gathering relevant information: Gathering relevant information is very important as there are always multiple factors involved in and affected by the problem.

Evaluating options: Evaluating the available options is the next logical step. Every problem has more than one solution, depending on the point of perception. Hence, all the possible options should be studied and evaluated as per the organization's baseline principles. The positive and negative consequences of all the options need to be weighed. At times, brainstorming with friends or colleagues may also help.

Many times, the situations are tricky and too many solutions seem to be staring at us. In such a scenario, there is no harm in taking time to think over the pros and cons and come to a logical conclusion.

Making decisions: A good leader is never tempted to make popular decisions; their decisions are always effective, even at the risk of being unpopular at times. In fact, corporate decisions, as many would have experienced, invariably involve some level of conflict or dissatisfaction to the other party. In the case of Krishna's decision about Mount Govardhan, Indra was the dissatisfied party.

As can be seen, following Krishna's systematic and very logical approach, we should be able to make the right decisions.

Krishna's timeless advice, 'Do not let your emotions make your decisions,' is not just a requirement but a cornerstone of every success story.

11.

Krishna on Justifiable Means

The end should justify the means.

An interesting way to explain 'justifiable means' is that it's a situation where an act, which may otherwise be deemed 'criminal', is made 'just' by the circumstances. A fitting example would be killing someone in self-defence.

In an organization, doing the right thing is not always straightforward. It may not necessarily be based on ethical principles; it may depend on the situation. What are ethical principles? They include the rights and duties of an organization and its employees, vendors and customers, and the fiduciary responsibility of its shareholders, if any.

An effective leader is expected to use justifiable means to achieve his ends. He cannot ignore the ethical principles. But the situations may not always turn out as desired, so the leader has to find a way around the ethical principles.

Unfortunately, all leaders are not genuinely effective. Some are cleverer and more effective for their own selves than their teams or organizations. Such a leader may seem sincere, intelligent, charming and even witty, but he may just be assessing what people want to hear and then making up stories to fit those expectations. These leaders are detrimental to the teams or organizations that they are leading, and result in meltdowns.

The global financial crisis of 2007–08 is a classic case attributed to the massive greed of banking and financial institutions. In a bid to attract homebuyers, these institutions indiscriminately approved mortgages. It spread like an epidemic. The credit-rating agencies also failed to evaluate the risks involved in mortgage-related financial products. It was like one rotten apple spoiling the entire basket.

During this financial crisis, the key people at the top of the world's largest banks came under scrutiny. The CEO of one of the banks that collapsed during this time was known for taking excessive risks with no concern for his own bank's mismanagement. He was unpredictable in his behaviour towards his colleagues and fostered a culture of fear. This eventually led to the bank's collapse.

Unfortunately, wrong leadership decisions can destroy the ethical standards of an organization. It is important to recognize such leaders before they destroy the organization itself.

Every leader faces ethical dilemmas and has to deal with them, keeping the larger picture in mind. Typically, when there is a conflict of values or when all alternatives are equally justifiable or when there are significant consequences for the greater good, an ethical dilemma will happen.

There is an incident on the battlefield of Kurukshetra when Arjun faces such an ethical dilemma. And, like always, Krishna helps him out of it.

In the battle of Kurukshetra, Karna was representing the Kauravas. He was a warrior par excellence, perhaps even better than the much-hyped Arjun of the Pandavas. While Arjun was the disciple of Guru Drona, Karna was the disciple of Drona's guru, Parashuram.

The two adversaries faced each other on the 17th day of the war. It was a 'do or die' moment for both.

Krishna, as Arjun's charioteer, was constantly motivating him to kill Karna. He did that by reminding Arjun how Karna killed his son Abhimanyu, and how he publicly insulted his wife Draupadi. Karna certainly did not deserve to live.

As the two arch-rivals fought, in the course of the battle, Karna shot a serpent arrow at Arjun. Instantly, Krishna, with his quick footwork, depressed the chariot into the ground, so that only the tip of Arjun's headgear broke off by the deadly arrow.

Filled with anger, Arjun was about to shoot his arrow at Karna, when he saw that the left wheel of Karna's chariot was jammed in the mud. Karna had to step down to free the wheel. Arjun allowed him to do so, since as per the rules of war, he was not supposed to strike his opponent until his vehicle was on the move again.

But Karna did not take Arjun's sense of duty for granted. He informed Arjun that he was under obligation to spare him while he was retrieving the wheel. This show of arrogance by Karna was not required and took an unfortunate turn for him.

It gave Krishna an opportunity to remind Karna of all the occasions when he neglected his obligations. Krishna's plan was to demoralize Karna and instigate Arjun to act.

Planning a fraudulent dice game between Yudhishthir and Duryodhan, insulting Draupadi in public, conspiring with Duryodhan to poison Bheem, encouraging Duryodhan to burn the Pandavas in Varanavat, being one of the warriors who killed an young, unarmed Abhimanyu, were some of Karna's misdeeds that Krishna now cited, asking him where his sense of duty was when he committed all these sins.

Karna was embarrassed. He had no answers.

Krishna's words had done the work of adding fuel to fire. Arjun's anger rose to such an extent that he didn't bother to wait for Karna's chariot wheel to be fixed. He took an aim and shot an arrow at Karna, killing him on the spot.

Some would say that it was unfair. Arjun broke the rule of the war. But then, to Arjun, it was fair. After all, Karna also broke the rule and attacked his unarmed son. And Krishna deliberately led him to that emotion, to evoke the desired action.

Next day, the 18th day, was the last day of the battle in Kurukshetra. With all the top-notch warriors dead, the Kauravas lost the war of Mahabharata to the Pandavas. As we can see, the killing of Karna was vital to the winning of the war by the Pandavas.

The end justified the means.

Work or business ethics stand for what is right or wrong in the workplace, and doing what is right in regard to its effect on the larger picture is a critical task for a leader. The decision not only affects the present performance of the organization, it also affects its growth in the future.

Learning and development are integral to growth. Team building, leadership and communication are popular topics for in-house workshops in any organization. Now ethics and compliance laws have also entered the picture, even creating places for Chief Ethics and Compliance Officers in large set-ups.

Most organizations normally have a code of ethics that is part of their policies. And like all laws, implementation or enforcement is the key. The biggest mistake that any leader can make is not to monitor and enforce their code of ethics. But then, there is another side to it. People can work around any laws; they can find loopholes to go through.

Keeping everything in mind, there are still some basic ethical values that are expected from leaders:

1. Honesty
2. Integrity
3. Trustworthiness
4. Loyalty
5. Fairness
6. Compassion
7. Respect
8. Accountability

Honesty: Leaders are expected to be truthful in their dealings. They are not expected to deliberately mislead or deceive others by showing a false picture of the reality.

Integrity: This is a step beyond honesty. The leaders are expected to adhere to the ethics of the organization without any compromise. Unscrupulous behaviour and hypocrisy are not expected from leaders.

Trustworthiness: This is a very important virtue in a leader. He is expected to be reliable, not only for the people above him in hierarchy, but also those below him in the chain. Leaders are expected to fulfil their promises and commitments.

Loyalty: This is expected in any relationship. A leader is expected not to disclose classified information about his organization to anyone outside of it. He is expected to respect the proprietary information of not just his current but also his former organizations. Loyalty as a generic trait is different from a person's current commitments. An effective leader may use the experience he has from his former engagements for his personal growth. But he should not use the information to benefit his current organization at the cost of his former organization. That would be unethical.

Fairness: It is very important for a leader to be fair to all, without showing any discrimination or favouritism. He is expected to be committed to mete out justice. Using power arbitrarily and taking advantage of another's mistake is not expected from a good leader. In fact, a leader is expected to admit when he is wrong, and change his opinion if required.

Compassion: A leader follows the golden rule, which is the principle of treating others as we would like to be treated ourselves. An effective leader is expected to accomplish the organization's objectives in a manner that causes least harm to others and the greatest good to all.

Respect: A leader is expected to treat everyone with equal respect and dignity, regardless of gender, religion or nationality. He is also expected to respect the privacy of his colleagues and subordinates.

Accountability: Like trustworthiness, accountability is also an integral part of leadership. An effective leader is expected to acknowledge and accept personal accountability for the outcomes of his decisions or omissions, to his team and organization.

Coming back to using justifiable means to achieve our objective—first, let us understand how it works. Humans engage in practical reasoning all the time. They plan and study about what to do and how to do it. Then they act in the light of reasons, which can explain their actions and also justify them. This action is called using justifiable means to achieve our objective.

There are two kinds of reasons behind human actions:

1. Normative
2. Motivating

Normative: These reasons are derived from the existing norms or codes that prescribe actions. A simple example would be norms of greeting in different countries dictating our actions there, like shaking hands in the UK and by pressing our palms together in namaste in India. Here, knowledge of the norms is needed to act, not any other thought or desire.

Motivating: A motivating reason would be one that provokes a person into action. It is a compelling emotion or desire that precipitates the action. In the case of Arjun, his anger against Karna motivated him to act. That this act resulted in Karna's death is another matter.

The job of a leader is to weigh the pros and cons of both and then decide on the action. After all, he is the one who has to be accountable for the consequences of his decisions and actions. He has to justify them.

Deciding what is right and what is wrong is tough. But then, that is what a great leader is all about. His reasons would always be justifiable.

But the toughest decision of all is between two 'rights'.

Sometimes the right thing for us may be wrong for someone else; it's a matter of perspective. When our children grow up and want to go out into the world to explore the various avenues to build their future, we tend to feel bad. As parents, we feel that it is wrong for children to leave their parents when they should be looking after them, as they themselves were looked after. But children feel otherwise. They feel that it is the right time for them to plan and work towards a bright future. By their perspective, the parents are wrong in pulling their children back. Who is right and who is wrong? Both are right by their own perspectives and both are wrong by the other's perspective. Each is seeing only one side. That doesn't mean that the other side doesn't exist.

Life is not black and white; it has shades of grey too.

Mahatma Gandhi said something very profound about being right and wrong. He said, 'When you are right, you have no need to be angry. When you are wrong, you have no right to be angry.'

It can be seen vividly in the anecdote mentioned earlier. Krishna knew he was right about his decision of setting the stage for Karna's death. He wasn't angry at all; it was Arjun who was angry. Karna realized that he had done wrong in the past. He was not angry; he was remorseful.

In one of his many works, Shakespeare wrote, 'Many times, to do a great right, we have to do a little wrong.' It encapsulates Krishna's theory of 'the end should justify the means.'

12

Krishna on Non-Justifiable Means

Some actions cannot be justified.

Justification focuses on beliefs. It is a common belief that every wrongdoing deserves to be punished. So punishing a wrongdoer would be justifiable anyway, provided one can prove that the doer did the deed.

An action in itself is not good or bad, the purpose is. An action is born out of two things:

1. Intent
2. Circumstances

Intent: If the intent of the action is good, then the action gets justified. Robin Hood was considered an outlaw by the government of his country. But he looted the rich and those who had amassed wealth by corrupt means and helped the poor with that money. His intent was good. His actions were justified.

Circumstances: Many times people are trapped by circumstances. If a male boss harasses his female employee regularly, a day will come when she's unable to take it any more. The next time, even if he just touches her without meaning any harm, she may just turn around and slap him hard. There are cases recorded in history where wives have shot dead their husbands' lovers on seeing them in compromising situations and vice versa. These people have committed crimes in a moment of heat, feeling cornered by circumstances. All crimes related to self-defence are also circumstantial. Here, there is no intent to do anything wrong, but circumstances push the person into doing wrong things. It is justified for them.

The various actions discussed above do not happen routinely, because then they cannot be justified. Robin Hood also was eventually caught and killed by his enemies. They justified their action as revenge.

Leaders can use non-justifiable means to attain their objectives, but sparingly. A regular user of such means becomes a psychopath. Studies have shown that about 4 per cent of corporate personnel are psychopaths, which is an alarming number.

To distinguish between an effective leader and a corporate psychopath, we need to observe the following three traits of the latter:

1. Interpersonal
2. Emotional
3. Lifestyle

Interpersonal: A corporate psychopath is charming and a glib talker. They get into good positions by using their charm and manipulating people. But the worst thing is that they are pathological liars and are good at covering up their misdeeds.

Emotional: These people are emotionally insensitive and

lack empathy towards others. Even after committing a wrong action, they do not feel any sense of guilt or remorse. In fact, they are quite good in pinning the blame on others for their own wrong acts.

Lifestyle: A corporate psychopath typically uses people to achieve his goals, even for his lifestyle needs. He prefers to live in the moment and has no realistic, long-term goals.

When such people handle leadership roles, their actions cause a ripple effect throughout the organization, affecting its corporate culture. This results in an increase in staff turnover, absenteeism, qualitative and quantitative reduction in productivity and a general dip in ethical standards of the organization. If unchecked, such an organization slides on to the path of self-destruction.

Duryodhan, the eldest Kaurava had the above traits, and as we know, these traits led him to the path of self-destruction. The only justification he had for all his actions was that he did not want Yudhishthir to get the crown of Hastinapur, which was non-justifiable in the eyes of the people.

But then, in the course of the great battle of Mahabharata, there was an incident where Krishna had to use non-justifiable means to achieve his objective. Let us see why.

The battle continued from the 14th day to the 15th, non-stop. Dronacharya, the teacher of the Kauravas and Pandavas, was leading the Kauravas. He had spread fear and destruction in the Pandava army by his relentless attacks.

Drona was the backbone of the Kaurava forces. His death was essential for the Pandavas' victory. But Arjun, the most capable Pandava warrior, was forbidden to kill him. The first reason was because Drona was a brahmin and killing a brahmin was a major sin in those times. And the second reason was that Drona was Arjun's teacher.

Krishna knew that none could defeat Drona fighting strictly according to the rules of war. So another way had to be devised.

Drishtadyumna, Arjun's brother-in-law, was leading the Pandava army. He was entrusted with the task of killing Drona. There was a reason behind the choice. His father Drupad had taken a vow to destroy Drona. As was common in those times, Drupad organized a huge, sacrificial fire and Drishtadyumna was born from that pit of fire. Since he was born for the purpose of killing Drona, he was safe from the sin of brahminicide. Even then, it was no mean task to do so.

Krishna told the Pandavas that the only thing that would make Drona vulnerable would be the death of his son Ashwatthama. 'If he hears that Ashwatthama is dead, Drona would lose all interest in life and would throw down his weapons. So somebody should go and tell him that his son has been killed,' he suggested.

Their brother Bheem went and killed an elephant named Ashwatthama. Then he went and announced loudly in the battlefield, 'I have killed Ashwatthama!'

Drona heard these words as he was about to launch a powerful missile to destroy the Pandava troops. He paused midway, stunned. Then he turned towards Yudhishthir, whose reputation for telling the truth surpassed even the gods. Drona asked Yudhishthir if the news of his son's death was genuine.

Yudhishthir responded, though nervously, 'Yes, it is true

that Ashwatthama has been killed...' And before he could add anything to it, Krishna blew his conch loudly and the drums started beating in the Pandava camp, completely drowning out Yudhishthir's next words, which were, '...Ashwatthama, the elephant.' Drona could not hear these words.

The news of his son's death broke Drona. He dropped all his weapons and sat down in his chariot, with his head bowed in sadness, praying.

Drishtadyumna seized this opportunity and rushed to Drona's chariot, brandishing his sword. Heedless of the cries of anguish all around, Drishtadyumna fulfilled his father's wish of beheading Drona.

Krishna's wish was fulfilled too. The objective was achieved, though by using non-justifiable means.

This is the quality of an effective leader, that he finds a way to achieve his target, even if by using non-justifiable means at times. However, the larger picture always manages to justify the leader's actions. In our story too, the larger picture of the Pandavas winning the war of Mahabharata, a victory of good over evil, justified everything.

Jonathan Kvanvig, a contemporary philosopher from Washington University, asserts that justification is not necessary in getting to the truth and avoiding errors. He says that knowledge is no more valuable than true belief.

What about the belief that the so-called law governing us is not just? History has seen many uprisings of people objecting to the rule of the land. Protests happen and rules are broken, all non-justifiable as per the lawmakers and rulers of that land.

It is important that we must know what we stand for, not

just what we stand against. Mahatma Gandhi also said, 'An unjust law is itself a species of violence. Arrest for its breach is more so.'

The fundamental question that arises here is, does the individual have the right to disobey the law when his mind or his conscience or his religious faith tells him that the law is unjust?

This question propels us to examine personal morality, civic obligation and the rules of the organization as well as the land. The words often used in this context are freedom, equality and independence. Resistance to an unjust rule or law is not just confined to revolutionaries or outlaws. It happens in corporate scenario as well. If the head of the organization or leader of the team are effective, they would discuss the reason for resistance with their subordinates or team, and iron out the situation. Differences of opinions between the CEO and the promoters of an organization are also not unheard of.

Many times the solutions seem unjust and the resistance turns into rebellion and escalates further into protest or some form of non-cooperation movement. The CEO may decide to do what he thinks is in the best interest of the organization, even if it means going against his promoters.

Of course, all this would be against the organization's policies and deemed illegal.

Any protestor's actions always seem non-justifiable to all others except him. When is it justified then for a person to act as his own legislator and to decide that he will or will not obey the given law? There is no perfect or single answer to this.

1. It is universally believed that if the boss is dictatorial then disobedience can sometimes be legit.
2. Disobedience or blatantly breaking the law may attract the attention of people who matter. Mahatma Gandhi and his supporters exemplified how civil disobedience can be used to make a point. It was an illegitimate act to make a legitimate point.
3. It is important to know that when we feel that we have the right to break the law, it cannot be a legal right under the law. It has to be a moral right against the law. And, most importantly, this moral right is not an unlimited right to disobey any law that we regard as unjust.
4. The exercise of the right to disobey law is subject to standards of just and moral behaviour. It cannot be a personal belief alone. It was not only Krishna who felt that Karna had done wrong. All who were witness to the incidents Krishna mentioned had felt that Karna had failed in his duty as a warrior and that he had sinned against the Pandavas.
5. Basic principles have to be at the core of the act. The wrong being combated has to be a serious one, one that would continue to grow if not fought against.
6. There should be reasonable grounds to believe that the otherwise legit method of fighting the wrong is insufficient by itself.

Krishna was not a habitual law-breaker. Though he was a warrior by birth, he preferred to resolve all issues by using peaceful means. But when these means failed, Krishna would not hesitate to pick up arms either.

KRISHNA ON NON-JUSTIFIABLE MEANS ▸ 115

In the case of Pandavas and Kauravas, when the latter refused to give the rightful share of property to the former, Krishna knew that a war was imminent. Even then, he wanted to try one last time to bring about a peaceful resolution to this problem. He personally went to meet the Kauravas and discuss across the table, so to speak, the various ways of bringing about peace between the two families. The discussion failed, the Kauravas were adamant on their stance, and war was declared.

Krishna even spoke to Karna. He knew how important Karna was to the Kauravas. But there also he met with disappointment. It seemed that none in the Kaurava camp were interested in any form of peace negotiations.

The only recourse left now was war. And since the Pandavas had a very small army as compared to the Kauravas, Krishna had to have his wits about him to guide them to fight cleverly with limited resources.

Being a warrior himself, Krishna knew the rules of war well. Like the great leader that he was, Krishna strategized within and sometimes around the rules to achieve his objective. After all, the person who knows the rules thoroughly also knows the loopholes to go through.

Using his skills of driving, Krishna drove as well as guided Arjun in the battlefield at every step. He encouraged him, comforted him and even scolded him if the situation so demanded. The ultimate objective was for the Pandavas to win the war.

Kauravas had the greatest of warriors leading their army. It would be a tactical move for the Pandavas to kill these commanders, to shake up the army. Drona was one such invincible commander. He was the teacher of the Kauravas as well as the Pandavas, and knew more about warfare than all of them put together. That was the reason why it was impossible to kill him in normal combat.

Krishna had to think out of the box. Standard combat strategies were useless in this situation. So Krishna had to look for a weak spot in his target. Having found one, it would be easy to breach in.

At this juncture of the war, no opportunity could be ignored to achieve the objective. So, once the weak spot was identified, the hit was made.

Though the act of killing Drona may be non-justifiable by the rulebook of the war, it led the Pandavas to their ultimate goal. Drona's death was unimaginable and the impact was as if the collective backbone of the Kauravas had been broken. Victory for the Pandavas was guaranteed now.

Krishna had no personal agenda. His objective for the greater good was to make the Pandavas win the battle of Mahabharata and make the righteous Yudhishthir king of the country. Using justifiable means at times and non-justifiable means at others, he achieved this objective.

As they say, all is fair in love and war.

13.

Krishna on Goals

Set goals; make the invisible visible.

The dictionary definition of a goal is the object of a person's ambition or effort; an aim or desired result. Basically, a goal is an idea of the desired future. It encompasses personal and professional future. Individuals may or may not, but every organization sets goals to work towards.

In fact, we are taught about goal setting in primary school, when we are told to write an essay about what we want to be when we grow up. And nobody wants us to forget that as we are growing, because that's what decides what subjects we take in high school, and subsequently in college. This question haunts us till we actually find a job. That is when other people stop bothering us with questions, but then some of us, if not all, start setting our own personal and professional goals.

In the words of Norman Vincent Peale, author of the bestseller *The Power of Positive Thinking*, 'All successful people have a goal. No one can get anywhere unless he knows where he wants to go and what he wants to be.'

There are three types of goals:

1. Topic based
2. Focus based
3. Time based

Topic based: Goals can be personal, professional, or financial. We could have a personal goal of losing weight or getting a particular diploma. Professional goals are related to our career path, about what we want to do for a living and where we want to reach in that. Saving money to buy property or just to have a nest are basic financial goals.

Focus based: This is a very singular goal, like writing a book or building a house. It can impact personal and professional goals.

Time based: Goals can be short-term like spring-cleaning the house or long-term like landscaping a garden. In an organization, a short-term goal could be to improve the national sales figures by 5 per cent in a quarter. The long-term goal could be to be one of the top three in the industry.

Whatever the type of goal, it should be specific, measurable and actionable. But, more often than not, many of us fail to achieve our goals. Why?

1. Fear of failure
2. Setting the goals for wrong reasons
3. Not setting the priorities right
4. Lacking a plan
5. Lacking commitment

Fear of failure: Fear of failing is very common and if we allow it to ride us, it destroys our self-confidence. The journey would be downhill from there.

Setting the goals for wrong reasons: Many times, we may set the goals that we see others setting, assuming they are right for us. Then we waste our time and energy in following those only to realize they are no good for us.

Not setting the priorities right: Our goal may be right but we may be going about it the wrong way. Prioritising is imperative to making any plan of action. Otherwise, we end up getting distracted and wasting time.

Lacking a plan: Setting a goal is of no use if there is no systematic plan of action to achieve it. If we fail to plan, we plan to fail. A plan is the path to our goal. It is like a GPS map that we use to drive from point A to point B.

Lacking commitment: Even with everything in place, if we lack commitment, we cannot achieve anything. We need to believe in our goal and the path we are taking to achieve it. If we are not committed to our goal and plan, we will not have the drive to work towards it, let alone achieve it. No job can be successfully executed half-heartedly.

So, we need to pull up our socks, set the right goal, make the appropriate plan and head towards achieving it with full faith in our goal and ourselves.

'Our goals can only be reached through a vehicle of plan, in which we must fervently believe, and upon which we must vigorously act. There is no other route to success,' said Pablo Picasso, the famous artist.

Let us see how Krishna achieved his goals.

Krishna first saw the Pandava brothers in the kingdom of Panchal, where Arjun won Princess Draupadi's hand. He followed them to where they were living with their mother Kunti in a small hut, on the outskirts of the city. Kunti was Krishna's aunt.

This was Krishna's first meeting with the Pandavas. He stayed back for their official wedding with Draupadi. Subsequently, he and Arjun became good friends.

Krishna's goal in life was to teach righteousness and to establish a kingdom based on the principles of righteousness. After meeting the Pandava brothers, he realized that Yudhishthir had all the desired qualities to run the country righteously.

From then on, Krishna started planning and strategizing to achieve his goal.

When the Pandavas reached Hastinapur with their new bride, they were received warmly. Their uncle, Dhritarashtra, gave them a land called Khandavprastha, which had once been ruled by their ancestors. Though the place was in shambles, the Pandavas happily accepted the land and set about renovating it.

Khandavprastha had a huge cover of forest that needed to be cleared to make land available for building the city. The common practice those days was to burn down the forests to clean up the land. That is what Arjun set out to do.

Krishna was visiting them and went along with Arjun to do this task. While they were setting the forest on fire, they met Maya Daanav, who was an architect possessing exceptional building skills. They spared his life and Maya offered to repay the duo by building something for them.

Arjun was not interested. But Krishna took advantage of the opportunity. He asked Maya to build a beautiful pavilion for Yudhishthir, to hold conferences with kings and other important people.

The grateful Maya built an exquisite pavilion for Yudhishthir. It was as beautiful as Indra's abode in heaven and since then, Khandavprastha began to be known as Indraprastha.

Krishna's desire of getting a magnificent pavilion or conference hall for Yudhishthir was his first step towards his goal. He wanted the kings of neighbouring kingdoms to visit Yudhishthir and hold meetings in the impressive hall. He wanted the kings to get to know Yudhishthir as the king of Indraprastha and pledge their allegiance to him.

Krishna was setting the stage for Yudhishthir to become the king of the entire Bharat, slowly but surely. He had set a goal and was now making the 'invisible visible'.

Once Yudhishthir was installed as king of Indraprastha, his fame started spreading far and wide. His subjects were happy, the kingdom was flourishing and there was no poverty or conflict in his domain. Yudhishthir as a righteous king had garnered a huge following, and some of those kings suggested that a Rajasuya yagya should be performed to declare Yudhishthir's popularity and might in the country.

The idea, which was seeded by Krishna, was now taking shape. Yudhishthir wanted Krishna's advice on the next step to be taken.

Krishna told him that the kings currently favouring him are not enough. Bharat was a big country. Jarasandh, the king of Magadh, had a hundred kings in his captivity. Killing him would release those kings, who would naturally favour and support Yudhishthir. The final number of supportive kings would increase substantially and then Yudhishthir could perform his yagya and claim to be the irrefutable emperor of the country.

The plan was good and was executed by Bheem, Arjun and Krishna. Bheem killed King Jarasandh. The hundred captive kings were freed and, as expected, pledged their allegiance to Yudhishthir. The Rajasuya yagya was conducted successfully and Yudhishthir was proclaimed the emperor.

This was the second step of Krishna towards achieving his goal. The invisible was no more so; it was quite visible now.

To accomplish our goals we need to know how to set them. Goal setting is a process that begins with careful consideration of what we want to accomplish, and goes through a series of well-defined steps, ending with a lot of hard work going into actually doing it.

There are four golden rules of goal setting:

1. Set goals that motivate us
2. Set SMART goals
3. Make an action plan
4. Keep tracking

Set goals that motivate us: Motivation is the key to achieving goals. Goal achievement requires commitment. So, to maximize the likelihood of success, we need to feel the value or importance of that goal in our life. A worthwhile goal would keep us motivated on the path of achieving it.

Set SMART goals: SMART as in Specific, Measurable, Attainable, Relevant and Time-bound.

The goal has to specific, clear and well defined. Since goals show us the way, we need to define precisely where we want to reach. The goal has to be measurable in terms of quantum, in order to measure its success. If we talk of reducing expenses or increasing profits, we need to know the quantum (percentage) of what we want.

The goals should be challenging yet attainable. Unrealistic goals or ones that are too easy to achieve should be avoided. The goals must be relevant to the larger purpose of our life. Finally, the goals must have a deadline.

Make an action plan: An action plan involves identifying, analysing and delegating tasks and resources to team members.

Keep tracking: Tracking is very important to keep the plan moving. Periodic monitoring helps to identify and iron out the problem areas.

'When it is obvious that the goals cannot be reached, don't adjust the goals, adjust the action steps,' advises Confucius wisely. At every stage of his plan, Krishna was quite flexible. He adjusted the plan according to the situation, because his goal was fixed.

But, if we set the goals and for whatever reasons fail to achieve them, what then?

It means that we need to revisit our strategies and approach. Failing to achieve goals is normal. In fact, some people have achieved phenomenal success after failure.

Steve Jobs bought Pixar after getting fired from Apple. It

changed his thinking completely and when he returned to Apple, he revolutionized the company, and the rest is history, as we know.

Another interesting example is Walt Disney. If he had not been fired from his job at a newspaper for lack of imagination, Mickey Mouse would not have been born. And Walt Disney as a brand would never have been created.

Failure is part of the journey, which we need to experience before we achieve success. It makes us appreciate success more.

Here are some things that we can do to snap out of the low state of mind after we face a failure:

1. Analyse the reason
2. Take a break
3. Question ourselves
4. Learn to do better
5. Reignite our desire
6. Restart

Analyse the reason: We should treat failure as feedback and ask ourselves why we failed. Was it lack of hard work, lack of time or maybe we overestimated ourselves? Unless we find the reason for failure, it cannot be resolved.

Take a break: Sometimes, it is important to get away and clear our mind. We should stand away from the situation and look at it from a distance to understand it better. And for that, taking a break and doing something totally different helps—a game of golf, a vacation, anything to totally distract the mind away from failure. Once that happens, we are able to see the situation with more clarity.

Question ourselves: We must question ourselves to check if we overestimated ourselves. This helps us get back on track. If we realize that doing the same thing again will bring the same result because the fault lay in our own capability, then we can focus on improving ourselves.

Learn to do better: Maybe our strategy was wrong. Working hard, alone, does not guarantee success. We should review our strategies, and maybe get a mentor on board. Learning from experienced people always helps.

Reignite our desire: We need to keep our energy going. We should ask ourselves why we want to achieve the goals we have set; and the answer will be our motivation. This has to be kept alive.

Restart: After a failure, once we have analysed the situation and learnt from it, we need to revise our strategy and start again. It is just like the computer; we upgrade and restart.

Bruce Lee once said, 'Defeat is a state of mind. No one is ever defeated until defeat has been accepted as reality.'

Set your goals high and don't stop till you get there, the invisible will become visible. Krishna proved it with his own life.

14.

Krishna on Personal Growth

Write your own story.

Personal growth encompasses improvement of awareness, development of potential, honing of talent, enhancement of quality of life and realization of aspirations.

It is a lifelong activity. We get trained formally in the educational institutions and informally at home and in our workplaces. And indisputably, life's experiences remain the primary training in personal growth.

It is a very old concept. The Greek philosopher Aristotle called personal growth practical wisdom, involving good judgment and practice of virtues, leading to happiness and prosperity.

Chinese philosopher Confucius said, 'The ancients who wished to illustrate illustrious virtue throughout the kingdom first ordered well their own states. Wishing to order well their states, they first regulated their families. Wishing to regulate their families, they first cultivated their persons. Wishing to cultivate their persons, they first rectified their hearts. Wishing to rectify their hearts, they first sought to be sincere in their thoughts. Wishing to be sincere in their thoughts, they first extended to the utmost their knowledge. Such extension of knowledge lay in the investigation of things.'

We can see that personal growth is not limited to superficial material growth; it goes much deeper than that.

As recently as 1999, management educator Peter Drucker said, 'We live in an age of unprecedented opportunity: if you've got ambition and smarts, you can rise to the top of your chosen profession, regardless of where you started out. But with opportunity comes responsibility. Companies today aren't managing their employees' careers; knowledge workers must, effectively, be their own chief executive officers. It's up to you to carve out your place, to know when to change course, and to keep yourself engaged and productive during a work life that may span some fifty years.'

Krishna said all this, way before the oldest philosopher or management guru in the world. He motivated Arjun and Yudhishthir to write their own stories, which they did and were quite successful too. Krishna advised Karna to do the same, but he did not listen, and his story ended tragically.

There are five reasons behind the failure of personal growth:

1. Not listening
2. Not being open to the ideas of others
3. Not being honest to self
4. Not helping others to develop
5. Not taking initiative

Not listening: Listening is not just hearing, it's much more. Good listening skills include being able to listen for content as well as for the emotion or the reason behind it. Effective listening is a critical ingredient for personal growth.

Not being open to the ideas of others: Many people have a knee-jerk reaction to any suggestion by anyone. They may believe that their ideas are always better, or else, they may think the other person to be impertinent to be giving a counter-idea to them. Reacting negatively to feedback discourages others to give any feedback at all, which is fine for the giver. But ultimately, this negative attitude throttles the personal growth of the person not listening, as he would never know where he's going wrong.

Not being honest to self: Being honest to yourself is not always easy. People find it difficult to accept certain facts about themselves, and they continue to deny or rationalize them. This is self-deception. We need to be honest to ourselves, accepting the issues that need to be resolved or changed. Accepting reality is crucial to personal growth. As children if we hadn't accepted that our handwriting was bad, we never would've worked upon improving it. It's pretty much the same in adult life too.

Not helping others to develop: It is a strange but true fact that development is contagious. Helping others to grow and develop helps us in our personal growth. As in nature, everything is symbiotic in human life too. When we become helpful, we suddenly find help coming to us from different, often unexpected, sources. It's worth a try!

Not taking initiative: This is common sense. No growth, personal or otherwise, can take place without our participation in it. We cannot and should not depend on others for our own personal growth. We have to take the initiative, grab the opportunities and write our own story.

During Krishna's time, the Indian subcontinent was divided into several small kingdoms. Their differences and constant clashes made the country weak. Krishna felt that a major war would help in bringing the various kingdoms together under one righteous ruler and thus having a unified country.

Krishna saw potential in Yudhishthir to rule the country righteously. Even Yudhishthir himself was not aware of that potential. He was a virtuous man, a loving husband, a protective brother and a dutiful son. But being a leader and ruling over people was an entirely different ball game.

Indraprastha was established with a bit of help from Krishna, and Yudhishthir became the ruler of that kingdom by default. It was Krishna's way of gently nudging Yudhishthir on his path, to write his own story.

While on the job, Yudhishthir realized that he could be a good king. The kings from neighbouring kingdoms validated this fact. Yudhishthir was an effective listener; he was a just ruler and helped the people of his kingdom prosper. This reflected in his own personal growth. The neighbouring kings pledged their allegiance to him.

Yudhishthir did not let success go to his head. He always consulted Krishna on important matters. Though Krishna was younger than him in years, Yudhishthir considered him to be older in wisdom.

When everyone around him, friends and family, pushed him to declare himself as the emperor of the country, Yudhishthir did not get tempted immediately. He asked Krishna for his advice. Knowing that he still did not have enough kings in his kitty, Krishna advised Yudhishthir to kill Jarasandh and get his hundred captive kings pledge their allegiance to him. Yudhishthir agreed. The plan worked.

We can see how Yudhishthir was paving his own path, writing his own story. Whenever he was in doubt, he tapped Krishna's wisdom.

When it became evident that the war between the Kauravas and the Pandavas was imminent, Krishna offered to visit the Kauravas one last time as an emissary of peace from the Pandavas. He did this because he wanted Yudhishthir, the head of the Pandava family, to be seen as a man of peace as opposed to Duryodhan of the Kauravas, who desired war.

Yudhishthir agreed to Krishna's offer, though he could have vetoed it easily. Why? Because as the king of Bharat, he knew he would have to be a harbinger of peace and justice to his people.

Krishna knew that Yudhishthir was not a great warrior and hence did not encourage him to fight. After all, the future king of Bharat had to be protected.

Arjun was one of the greatest warriors of that time. Krishna helped him to direct his energies to the war at hand, the great battle of Mahabharata.

Standing in the middle of the battlefield, facing his cousins the Kauravas and his other relatives, teachers and friends, Arjun wanted to quit. Fortunately, Krishna was right there as Arjun's charioteer. He explained what the duties of a warrior were and that whether Arjun liked it or not, he was duty-bound to fight. Killing and getting killed in the line of duty was what a warrior did. Running away from the battlefield was not only cowardice but also a sin. This is how soldiers fight even today.

Arjun found his path and wrote his own story thereafter.

Krishna was a great warrior himself, but he did not pick up arms in the battle of Mahabharata. He wanted Arjun to realize his own potential. All through the raging battle, Krishna encouraged Arjun with his words while driving his chariot dextrously. Arjun fought his own war, literally and figuratively.

Arjun had to win the war in order to make his elder brother Yudhishthir the king of Bharat. This he did. He wrote his story well.

On his way back from the peace mission of visiting the Kauravas, Krishna spoke to Duryodhan's friend Karna. He spoke about Karna's real mother being the Pandavas' mother Kunti, which actually made him a Pandava too. Krishna advised Karna to join the Pandava forces. But Karna did not take the advice. He had planned his own story already. He had pledged his allegiance to Duryodhan and saw no reason to back out from that. After all, he was a warrior too and knew that breaking a pledge was a sin. Karna knew that his story would not have a happy ending, but then that was his story.

Karna died in the battlefield, but he lived forever in people's hearts. He was a generous man, one of the greatest warriors of his time, a dutiful son to his foster parents and a loyal friend to Duryodhan. Karna rose from the ranks. He was the adopted son of a charioteer, but he managed to learn archery and warfare from the best of the teachers and his warring skills got him a place in Duryodhan's heart. Duryodhan made Karna the king of Anga. This was Karna's personal growth curve.

One thing is clear from observing the above people: We have to pave our own path for our personal growth, whether or not we have a 'Krishna' to help us. We have to write our story ourselves, as Ralph Waldo Emerson puts beautifully, 'The only person you are destined to become is the person you decide to be.'

Let us see how we can jumpstart our personal growth:

1. Absorb
2. Use
3. Review
4. Act
5. Share

Absorb: We should learn to absorb everything that is happening around us, like a sponge. It is an extension of effective listening. If we pay attention and take in our surroundings, we will find that each moment, each day, teaches us something. All that wealth of learning helps us in our personal growth.

Use: Success is not just knowledge; it is how we use that knowledge effectively for the larger good. Success is also not just experiences; it is what we learn from those experiences and how we utilize that learning to improve things. The ability to put our knowledge and experiences to good use is one of the key factors in our personal growth.

Review: If we make time in our busy schedules simply for reviewing, we would learn not to repeat certain mistakes and probably even change our current decision for the better. It is like how, at the end of the year, we review the year gone by, learn from its mistakes and make resolutions for a better life in the coming year. In an organization, too, the financial year-ending reports play a crucial role in planning the coming year's production and sales targets.

Act: This one is simple. What would be the point of dreaming or making plans if we do not act upon them? Krishna planned to make Yudhishthir the king of Bharat. Then he set about acting on that plan, making strategies for its execution. The result was there for all to see.

Share: This is related to helping others develop. When we share our knowledge to help others grow, unknowingly we are helping ourselves to grow as well. As we teach or share, we tend to revise and go over our own knowledge. As we go along, we learn the mistakes we should not repeat and the decisions we should not take—this review, though unintentional, helps us in our personal growth.

But before we jumpstart, let us first confirm that we have the requisite mindset for personal growth. The checklist is:

1. Justifying actions
2. Engaging with people
3. Dreaming
4. Dealing with failure

Justifying actions: First of all, we need to stop justifying all our desires and actions to people around us. Our personal growth is our personal matter; we are not answerable to anyone for it. We must learn to say, 'I am doing this because I want to.'

Engaging with people: It is important to meet people other than those who share our interests. It opens up our minds, broadens our views and stimulates creativity. A plant cannot bloom inside a closed box. Our brain is like that; it needs stimulation to bloom to its full capacity.

Dreaming: The main point to remember is that the greatest things of life started out as a dream. As Walt Disney said, 'If you can dream it, you can do it.' We should treat our dreams as our goals and start planning to accomplish them.

Dealing with failure: Failure is part of success; it's like the other side of the coin. Not every plan is an instant or sureshot success. We may fail. It is normal. But we have to learn to try again. As Buddha says, 'In the confrontation between the stream and the rock, the stream always wins, not through strength, but through persistence.'

Once we have ticked off the checklist above and concluded that we have the requisite mindset for personal growth, half the job is done. It is like preparing the field for sowing seeds.

To jumpstart our journey towards personal growth, we just have to sow the seeds mentioned earlier: absorb, use, review, act and share. With careful tending of these characters and habits that we have imbibed, our personal growth chart will surely start showing an upward trend.

This is how simple it is to write our own story, according to Krishna.

15.

Krishna on Vision Statement

Vision is the art of seeing what is invisible.

The vision of an organization is its goal, which attracts and motivates its employees. A vision statement is the organization's roadmap towards its goal. It sets a defined direction for the organization's growth.

A vision statement is what we return to whenever we get confused about our main goal. It is like the pole star for an organization.

Let us see the vision statements of some well-known companies.

Sports shoe company Nike's vision statement is: *Bring inspiration and innovation to every athlete* in the world. (*If you have a body, you are an athlete.)*

The vision is motivational.

Computer giant Microsoft's vision statement is: *There will be a personal computer on every desk running Microsoft software.*

The vision is clear and precise.

Fast food chain McDonalds' vision statement is: *To be the best quick service restaurant experience. Being the best means providing outstanding quality, service, cleanliness and value, so that we make every customer in every restaurant smile.*

The vision statement marks the roadmap to success with signposts.

An organization's vision statement is thus an articulation of its main goals and ambitions.

An organization that does not have a vision statement may not fail, but will certainly not grow to its full potential. Growth, expansion and improvement need to be directed, in the general direction of the goal or vision of the organization. Some organizations may have vision statements, yet they fail. Why?

There are four main reasons:

1. Lack of clarity
2. Lack of focus
3. Lack of unity
4. Lack of perseverance

Lack of clarity: If the vision is generic and vague, it would have all the chances to fail. An organization's product, say a desktop printer, becoming successful in the market is a generic goal. But the product becoming one of the top two choices of the customer is a clear-cut goal.

Lack of focus: This is an extension of having lack of clarity. Focus leads a person to his goal. And this focus has to be present at all times, so that we do not get distracted from our goal. In the above example, making the desktop printer the hottest-selling one in the market should be the constant focus.

Lack of unity: Unity provides strength. A group of people, united in their purpose, can achieve much more than double the number of people but dissimilar in their thinking. 'United we stand, divided we fall' is applicable in organizations too.

Lack of perseverance: Many times, patience and endurance are needed to pull through a task. People who give up at the slightest obstacle or challenge are the ones who bring themselves and their organizations down.

Robert Greenleaf, founder of Servant Leadership movement, explains the vision statement well, 'The statement of vision is the overarching purpose, the big dream, the visionary concept—something presently out of reach—so stated that it excites the imagination and challenges people to work for something they do not yet know how to do.'

The key phrases to be noted are 'big dream' and 'presently out of reach'—the leader sees the invisible. He has the capacity to translate this invisible into visible, into reality.

Krishna's vision was to establish a righteous rule in a unified Indian subcontinent. He gathered like-minded people in his support and moved steadfastly towards that goal, making and changing strategies depending on the demands of the situations, as he went along.

Krishna's vision was so clear that the war of Mahabharata was visible to him, when it was invisible to the rest of the world.

The Pandavas spent 12 years in exile and a year incognito as penalty for losing in the fraudulent dice game with their cousins, the Kauravas. After fulfilling all the conditions of penalty, they asked for their share of inheritance from the Kauravas.

The Kauravas refused to part with anything, provoking

the Pandavas to fight for their inheritance.

In those times, there were no formal courts of justice. The elders sat together to discuss the matters and reach a verdict to everyone's satisfaction. Thus, the matter of inheritance was discussed amongst the elders of the Pandava family, their relatives and friends.

Krishna was also a part of the discussion. He urged everyone to find a solution that would be in the best interests of the Pandavas as well as the Kauravas. He supported Yudhishthir's proposal of pleading for only five villages, in case the Kauravas remained adamant on not returning the original land of the Pandavas.

Krishna wanted righteousness to prevail. His vision was clear. For him, the important fact was that a person was cheating another and this needed to be stopped. The quantum of land was not important. And he preferred to use peaceful means to settle disputes.

Emissaries were sent back and forth from the Pandavas to the Kauravas and vice versa. There was a deadlock. The Kauravas refused to part with anything. Finally, as a last attempt for peace and for the good of people at large, Krishna decided to meet the Kauravas as an emissary of peace from the Pandavas.

Krishna was interested in the well-being of both the families. He wanted to avoid the bloodshed of innumerable people. He was batting for the common good.

As Krishna was leaving for Hastinapur, the capital of the Kauravas, Draupadi met him on the way. With tears of anger in her eyes, she said, 'To not kill someone who deserves to be slaughtered, is as much sin as killing a person who did not deserve to die. My heart has been burning in anger for the past 13 years. I cannot forget or forgive Duhshasan for pulling my hair and dragging me to be disrobed in public. This talk of peace that you all are indulging in is breaking my heart. I demand justice!'

Though Krishna spoke about avoiding violence, he could clearly see a great war happening, and that too, soon. And in that war, he could also see the victory of the righteous Pandavas.

He consoled Draupadi, 'Wipe your tears. Within a few days you will find the Kaurava ladies in tears. They would be mourning their dead male relatives. Under the leadership of Yudhishthir, we will destroy the Kauravas. Soon you will see your husbands winning back their kingdom, and more, after slaying their enemies.' Krishna was confident.

Thereafter, he proceeded for the Kaurava court to campaign for peace even though he saw what the future held. Krishna knew for sure that Duryodhan would never agree to share even a small part of his kingdom to bring about peace. Yet he was going to meet him.

Why? Because Krishna believed that whatever needed to be done should be attempted even if it did not lead to success.

It is worth noting here that since Krishna had planned to make Yudhishthir the king of a unified Bharat, he always projected him as a leader. We can clearly see how Krishna was moving towards his vision.

Once he reached Hastinapur, Krishna did not go to the Kaurava court right away with his proposal of peace. He first met all the elders of the Kaurava clan and went to meet Kunti, his paternal aunt and mother of the Pandavas.

Kunti met Krishna and burst into tears, remembering how her sons and daughter-in-law suffered during their exile. Krishna consoled her by saying, 'Your sons are enjoying the pleasures of being brave.' And assured her further that she would soon find her sons victorious and prosperous.

Krishna was seeing the unseen; he was seeing the victory of righteousness over sinfulness.

Krishna spent the night at Vidur's home. Vidur was the stepbrother of Dhritarashtra, the king of Hastinapur. Vidur told Krishna sadly that his peace mission was doomed, because Duryodhan would never compromise. Unfortunately, his father Dhritarashtra was silent on the matter, which was construed as his support.

Krishna explained that the person who does not try to prevent division between his relatives couldn't be considered as a relative. He had come to give Duryodhan good advice, as was his duty towards his kin. Whether that advice would be taken or not, was not Krishna's responsibility.

Next day, Krishna did what he had come to do. His offer was rejected, as was expected. The war of Mahabharata was declared between the Kauravas and the Pandavas. The story moved on. The invisible was now becoming visible to all.

Krishna's journey continued on the path leading to his goal of unifying the country and installing a righteous ruler to govern it.

Observing Krishna, we can arrive at the following five essentials for an effective vision statement:

1. Should be ambitious
2. Should be clear

3. Should be inspirational
4. Should be realistic
5. Should be consistent

Should be ambitious: Our vision statement has to be ambitious if we want to grow and flourish in life. A stagnant organization eventually disintegrates into oblivion. The first step in establishing any organization is to give it an ambitious goal to achieve. Krishna's vision was also ambitious when he started out. Considering that he met Yudhishthir for the first time and identified him as the ruler of a unified Indian subcontinent in future—it was an ambitious goal indeed!

Should be clear: This is also simple. Without clarity of vision, how can one proceed? Krishna had absolute clarity about what he wanted. That clarity guided him at every step. Diversions would keep coming, but if our goal is clear, we would always be able to keep an eye on it. And that would help us to stick to the right path. It is like following the pole star. The star is so clear and bright that no one following it can ever get lost.

Should be inspirational: The vision statement should challenge, enthuse and inspire those who are following it. People working in an organization should be convinced of its vision and how it would be beneficial for them and good for everyone in general. Only then would a synergy be created and the action would happen. Synergy comes from like-minded people getting together. Krishna's vision of establishing a righteous rule was of obvious benefit to the people at large.

Should be realistic: Though sounding contradictory, a vision can be ambitious as well as realistic. One needs to find a balance here. The trick is to see what is doable and then jack it up a couple of notches. Krishna's vision of having a righteous rule was doable. Then he met the Pandavas and identified Yudhishthir as the future king. Since there were only five Pandava brothers, Krishna had to increase their forces. His vision became ambitious but was also realistic. The end result was seen by all.

Should be consistent: An organization's vision should be consistent, like Krishna's was. All his paths led to his vision of a righteous rule in the country. A vision statement is like a roadmap: The destination is clear but the route may change according to situations one might face on the way, quite like the GPS rerouting to avoid congestion on the way. If Krishna's path to getting the righteous Yudhishthir to rule over a unified country had to pass through the battlefield of Kurukshetra, so be it. The battle was fought and won.

Management guru Mark Lipton summarizes, 'A vision is successful when it "speaks" to a wide audience, tells an engaging story that people want to be a part of, challenges people, and creates a sense of urgency. Success occurs when the vision becomes embedded in the daily decisions and actions taken of those you want to lead. When we see a vision that is working, guiding an organization to sustained growth, we know that behind it are leaders who are comfortable leading with their hearts as well as their heads.'

Clearly, Krishna led with both his head and heart.

For an effective leader of an organization, setting a vision statement is not enough. Their job is to constantly work on improving themselves and their team. So, how do we improve ourselves?

1. *By spending more time with clients or customers.* It would give an insight on what they want and what we are giving and also what is available to them from other sources.
2. *By analysing the competitors.* It is very important to know our competitors, their strengths and weaknesses. We need to understand the reasons behind the success of all our competitors.
3. *By studying global trends.* Devouring as much information as possible related to industry trends keeps us up to date and helps us to compete better.

Following Krishna's footsteps wouldn't be a bad idea either.

16.

Krishna on Karma

Duty before self works in every situation.

Karma literally means action, work or deed.

Karma also refers to the spiritual principle of cause and effect, where the intent and actions of a person influence the future of that person. This is the essence of the Law of Karma or the Karma theory.

Krishna talks about karma as related to work. He says, 'Your work is your responsibility, its result is not. Never let the fruits of your action become your motive. Nor give in to inaction. Remain even-minded in success, and in failure. Even-mindedness is true yoga.'

This path of selfless action is called karma yoga.

From here comes the concept of duty or responsibility being a moral or legal obligation. According to Krishna, we should perform our duties selflessly. He exemplified karma yoga himself. He lived a worldly life but never abandoned his duty to uphold righteousness and protect the world from sinfulness. Eventually, he supported the Pandavas to fight the battle against the evil forces of the Kauravas to restore righteousness in the world.

Krishna himself had no stake in the war; he was not benefitting personally from it. He participated in the war to teach people the principles of karma yoga. But look at the larger picture: He had transformed his vision into reality. This is the main thing in management and in being a leader—we have to accomplish our goal.

In an organization, the responsibilities are distributed amongst employees. They are slotted into departments like administration, operations, marketing, distribution/sales, finance, human resource development, public relations, housekeeping, and so on. As per karma yoga, everyone has to do the duties assigned to them, diligently. Their focus should be on their own duty and not what other people are doing or not doing or how they are doing it. The homeostasis is not to be disturbed. This is also called teamwork. Everyone does their own bit as their contribution to the larger picture, their goal.

When we go to a doctor, his duty is to check us, make a diagnosis and prescribe treatment. He has to perform his duty with commitment and diligence. As a patient, we have to follow our doctor's prescription sincerely. Then there are other factors like our age, willpower, diet and environmental factors, which have a role to play in our getting well. We can clearly see from this that it's not doctor alone who cures a patient. A favourite phrase with the doctors is, 'We do our best, and God does the rest.'

If doctors start getting overly attached to the fruit of their actions, which is that patients should be cured, what would happen if a patient doesn't get cured, or dies? The treating doctor would feel guilty. And considering the number of patients any doctor sees in his career, he would probably be burdened by guilt very early in his life. It will affect his performance and naturally his patients. The larger purpose of him becoming a doctor to heal patients would be defeated

The same holds true if a salesman is only interested in increasing his number of sales, thus eyeing the commission rather than the customer he is selling to. The success of a product depends on customer satisfaction. If the customer is not satisfied, the sales would dwindle after some time. Often it is seen that overzealous salespeople have ruined the reputations of their organizations. They focus only on their own reward and nothing else.

As Ramakrishna, the great mystic, says, 'To work without attachment is to work without the expectation of reward or fear of any punishment.' And to repeat Krishna, 'Your work is your responsibility, the result is not. Never let the fruits of your action become your motive.'

Ever wondered what keeps us away from success? There are ten reasons that stand out very clearly:

1. Procrastination
2. Avoidance
3. Distractions
4. Underestimation
5. Overjustification
6. Perfectionism
7. Ineffective strategies
8. Impatience
9. Inflexibility
10. Introversion

Procrastination: Some of us have the tendency to put off things till the last moment. Buying tickets for an important trip, getting medical insurance done, fixing a leak in the kitchen plumbing—there are many such familiar examples where, if we do not act on time, we suffer loss. Likewise at work, decisions always need to be taken at the right time. Late decisions and late actions can result in loss of contracts, loss of credibility in the market and a general slowdown of business. We must always keep in mind that procrastination makes easy things hard, and hard things harder. Pablo Picasso puts it very beautifully, 'Only put off until tomorrow what you are willing to die left undone.'

Avoidance: If the task is not something we like doing, we tend to avoid it. Like if we need to meet the CEO of another organization, and we don't like him as a person, we try to postpone the meeting. But this cannot work if the meeting is vital to a decision related to our own organization.

Distractions: Focus on the goal is very important if we want to reach it. The world is full of distractions, but we have to steer clear of them and not lose sight of our goal. Good deals may come our way to tempt us, but we need to see how they gel with our own vision and action plan. Diversions on the way slow us down and ultimately take us away from our original goal.

Underestimation: It may happen that we have underestimated our goal and therefore our strategies may turn out to be ineffective. The only way out from such a miscalculation is to monitor the plan regularly and have resources on standby.

Overjustification: Some people do not like to be told that they might be doing something wrong, even by well-wishers. They would try to justify their actions by every means, arguing that they can't possibly go wrong. This premise itself is wrong. Nobody is infallible. We should spend less time in justifying our mistakes and more in finding solutions.

Perfectionism: Perfectionism may over complicate a simple task and make it difficult to attain. Trying to get every little point covered in a contract may result in it slipping away from our hands. Keeping it short and simple works for corporate goals too. Julia Cameron makes a very valid and thought-provoking point on perfectionism: 'Perfectionism is not a quest for the best. It is the pursuit of the worst in ourselves, the part that tells us that nothing we do will ever be good enough, that we should try harder.'

Ineffective strategies: It is not necessary to get the right strategy in place in the very first instant. If we see that we are not getting what we want, it is time to change what we are doing. Hard work may turn out ineffective if the strategy for its application is wrong. Changing strategy midway is not wrong. We must also observe and learn from those who have achieved the results that we want; maybe they are doing something that we have missed out completely.

Impatience: To achieve our goals, we need to have drive as well as patience. We can't sow a seed and pull it out after every couple of days to check if the roots have come out or not. Things take time to happen. Once the ball is set in motion, it will reach its goal. Every goal has its set of obstacles we need to persevere and continue on our path.

Inflexibility: People misconstrue being flexible for being weak; it is not so. In fact, it is the other way round. If a plan is not working, it should be changed. If the methods are obsolete, they should be changed. The goal remaining the same, we can certainly change the path if we get stuck on the original one. Rerouting should be allowed to happen.

Introversion: Many people are so obsessed with their work that they only read literature related to their field of interest, make friends with those doing the same kind of work, and do not socialize much. This is stagnation. We must meet successful, driven people from various fields. It will help us to grow and see things with a different perspective.

All the above ten reasons are purely self-created. And since we create them, we can destroy them easily too. Albert Einstein once said, 'The measure of intelligence is the ability to change.' If success is deluding us, we must pause, revisit our plan and change it for the better.

In the Mahabharata, the first time Krishna spoke about karma was when Sanjay, an emissary from the Kaurava king Dhritarashtra, went to tell the Pandavas to desist from any form of rivalry with their cousins. Basically, Dhritarashtra knew that war would not be good for the Kauravas. So, in response to the Pandavas' request for their rightful inheritance, the Kaurava king sent Sanjay to dissuade them.

Sanjay told Yudhishthir that Dhritarashtra's sons were wicked and would not agree to part with anything. But then the Pandavas should think before taking a huge step like that of a war. 'Can happiness be gained with possessions gained through war? What good can we reap from a kingdom won after killing our own relatives?' Sanjay asked Yudhishthir. 'If

Duryodhan and his brothers are fools, does it mean that you should also leave the path of righteousness and start a war?'

Krishna retorted to this, 'As warriors, the Pandavas are performing their sacred duty to protect their property. The Kauravas, also warriors, are obstructing the Pandavas from performing their duty of regaining their rightful property. Now, if the Pandavas can regain their kingdom by means other than war, it would be good and they still would be performing their duty. However, it would be fine if they engage in war and die fighting for their duty. You are asking them to reach a compromise and probably give up the idea of war. But, what would be dutiful for a warrior—daring to be in a just war or abandoning it? Who is leaving the path of righteousness here?'

Sanjay knew the answer, of course, but was helpless, as he was just an emissary.

Krishna then decided it would be better if he went to Hastinapur and met the Kauravas himself, with the last proposal of peace from the Pandavas.

Mahatama Gandhi had also said, 'Non-cooperation with evil is as much a duty as is cooperation with good.' And he did manage to free India from British rule, with his persistent non-cooperation movements.

The second instance of Krishna talking about karma is to Arjun on the battlefield of Kurukshetra. When Arjun saw all his cousins, teachers and other relatives standing in front of him ready for war, he was deeply anguished. He didn't want to kill them. He would have rather left the material world and become a hermit in the forests.

Krishna told Arjun, 'You have a right to perform your

prescribed duty, but you are not entitled to the fruits of your action. Never consider yourself as the cause of the result of your action and never be attached to not doing your duty.'

Krishna advised Arjun to fight as a matter of duty without attachment to its result. Because not only direct action but other known and unknown factors of the world also indirectly affect the outcome, and may give a totally unexpected result. This is an undeniable and unavoidable fact. So, one should ever be ready for any result. One can hope for the best, but should be prepared for the worst. When we act with this understanding, success and failure lose their capacity to shake us. We do not react, because we are not caught unawares. This equanimity is the essence of Krishna's karma yoga.

Karma yoga is not about forfeiting desires or emotions; it talks of actions driven by dispassion and level-headedness, avoiding anger, fear, attachment, arrogance or any other extreme emotion.

Arjun was attached to his relatives, teachers and friends, which was why he could not bear the thought of killing them. Hence it was important for him to understand the meaning of karma yoga. As a warrior, Arjun had a duty to perform. He had to fight for the larger goal, the goal of righteousness. His personal goals and issues were irrelevant at this moment.

Arjun's wanting to quit the war and leave the battlefield would have amounted to his not discharging his duty as a warrior. Not only is it cowardice, but it is also a sin.

Arjun realized his responsibility as a warrior and fought like one. Understanding karma yoga made him win the war for the Pandavas and accomplish the goal set by Krishna.

But how does Krishna's 'duty before self' help in a corporate scenario? How does it help us to become great leaders?

1. By serving our followers
2. By being where the action is
3. By being fair

By serving our followers: Selflessness is about strength. It is not for the weak. A weak leader would take the path of least resistance. He would claim all the credit for a job well done and none of the blame for any mishap. Real strength is how we enable our followers to accomplish success, without pressurizing them with any demands.

By being where the action is: This does not mean micromanaging or doing other people's jobs. It means to be there to listen to our subordinates, to understand what they need from us.

By being fair: It is important to ask ourselves if we are making our subordinates do things that we would be unwilling to do ourselves. We should not hope for success if we are pushing people against their wishes. Our plan should be one that we would want to execute ourselves; this feeling would filter down to our subordinates and encourage them to perform. No task can be successful if one's heart is not in it.

Warren Buffet, one of the world's greatest and most successful corporate leaders, discovered early in life that the more successfully we forget our selfish motivations, the more successful we become.

Great leaders are selfless. They understand that the power

they have is not about them. It is to ensure the benefit of the people they lead. They facilitate the success of others. Great leaders make people feel valued. In their presence people not only get inspired about the worthiness of the cause, but also understand their own worth. This is Krishna's principle of 'duty before self'.

Krishna had no vested interest in the goal that he had set for himself. He made Yudhishthir understand his worth as a righteous king, and Arjun his worth as the unconquerable warrior in the world.

While teaching the path of karma, Krishna was also following the same. As usual, he was teaching by his own example.

17.

Krishna on Work Etiquette

Success is measured by how you get along with people.

Work etiquette is the code of conduct governing social behaviour at a workplace. It creates a professional, mutually respectful atmosphere and improves communication, resulting in enhanced productivity.

Workplaces differ, so do certain aspects of work etiquette according to the place and people. But the basics remain the same. If we do not follow the basic rules of workplace etiquette, we not only become exceedingly unpopular but our professional growth also could be hampered.

Poor etiquette spreads like wildfire. Lack of self-control in one person influences others and soon the entire team loses a sense of discipline, resulting in loss of productivity.

Some don'ts to be kept in mind are:

1. Not to adopt a casual attitude towards work
2. Not to invade the privacy of others
3. Not to talk too much
4. Not to talk loudly
5. Not to indulge in office gossip
6. Not to interfere
7. Not to be late for work

8. Not to be sloppy
9. Not to brag
10. Not to complain often
11. Not to lose control
12. Not to use bad language
13. Not to forget decorum

Not to adopt a casual attitude towards work. The organization pays us for working hard towards its goal, and not for wasting our time. Time is money, as they say. Wasting someone else's time is unprofessional, and wasting our own time is foolish.

Not to invade the privacy of others. We should not touch or open anyone else's computer, drawers, or files. And we should always knock before entering anyone's cabin. What we give is what we get. We have to respect others' privacy for them to respect ours.

Not to talk too much. Talking too much entertains only the talker and not the listener. Talkative people waste their own time as well others' and hence are not appreciated in any workplace.

Not to talk loudly. Talking loudly whether on the phone or otherwise is very disturbing to fellow workers. A loud voice is an asset only when one is performing on stage, not in a workplace.

Not to indulge in office gossip. We would not like people to talk about us behind our backs, so we should also refrain from doing so. We should steer clear from office politics and blame games

Not to interfere. We should never interfere in anyone's affairs, whether personal or work related. It invariably leads to misunderstandings. The line between professional and personal relationship should not be breached.

Not to be late for work. It is important to maintain the discipline of the organization. Reaching late for work and taking unnecessary leaves should be avoided. Reaching late for an appointment indicates lack of respect for the person one is meeting. This does not augur well in a professional scenario.

Not to be sloppy. This is applicable to our workstation as well as our own selves. We should always keep our workstation neat and clean; a messed-up place results in messed-up thoughts. And also, we should dress well for work. An employee is the face of the organization, so we should present our best.

Not to brag. Nobody likes a braggart. Instead of blowing our own trumpet, the better way to celebrate our success would be to take our colleagues out for coffee. Someone has said, 'Our houses might be bigger than others', but our graves would be of the same size.'

Not to complain often. Some people have a habit of complaining about every little thing that is not to their satisfaction. This attracts attention to the negative things in the workplace and disturbs others. The better thing would to be to get the problem resolved by the concerned person, instead of making a big issue out of it.

Not to lose control. Many occasions test our patience in our workplace, but we need to maintain our balance through it all. Strong emotions like anger, hatred, jealousy or even love can cloud our judgment. Good leaders are always in control of their emotions.

Not to use bad language. Bad language is never appreciated in any workplace. Our language is a reflection of our own character. Using bad language actually makes a person lose respect in the eyes of the listener.

Not to forget decorum. Some people get too comfortable too fast and become informal. In a workplace, we always need to remember the lines of hierarchy and maintain appropriate decorum.

Observing work etiquette is the one thing that makes us popular, or not. And our popularity is the index to our success.

Going by this, Krishna must be the most successful god ever, considering he was certainly the most popular.

During his childhood, Krishna caused a couple of demons to die, as they were threatening to kill him. But his becoming popular at that phase of life was based more on the fact that he was a very naughty yet lovable child.

Later on, in his adolescent years, Krishna started actively protecting the people of his town from all kinds of problems. Once, he got rid of a huge snake that was poisoning their river. Water is the lifeblood of living beings, so one can imagine how, if the source of water gets poisoned, all the plants and animals in the region must suffer and how difficult it must get for the survival of the townspeople.

Krishna fought with the snake and convinced him to move away with his family to another place.

People live with false beliefs, which tend to become rituals and continue forever. Krishna broke one such myth that his townspeople blindly believed in. He proved to them that Lord Indra was not responsible for the rains. It was nature's water cycle that brought about rains. The breaking of this myth saved the people from a lot of unnecessary waste of grains and other foods in the various rituals that they used to conduct to propitiate Lord Indra. Krishna taught his people the value of nature and how to look after it.

Such actions of Krishna made him a leader of sorts to his people. He developed a large following, which continued to grow unabated all through his life as his wisdom unfolded.

Krishna had one goal in his life—to establish a righteous rule over a unified Bharat. He had no personal ambitions of becoming a king himself, though he got plenty of opportunities to do so. He would always help in slaying the evil kings and install the rightful rulers back on their thrones. It's impossible for a selfless person like him to not be popular. And that is why the people of his own kingdom considered him as their leader, though their king was someone else.

When Krishna went to meet the Kauravas as the peace emissary of the Pandavas, on the way he met the local people and spent time with them. All had heard of Krishna's wisdom and naturally wanted to reach out to him. And as it's with any leader or celebrity, not everyone is able to meet them. Hence, Krishna took this opportunity of mingling with the locals and chatting with them.

Novelist Maya Angelou has rightly observed, 'People will forget what you said, people will forget what you did, but people will never forget how you made them feel.' This is a vital aspect of work etiquette. Krishna treated everyone with respect; they could discuss their problems with him without any hesitation, knowing that he would advise them well. Krishna never talked down to anyone; he always talked with them. This was one of the reasons behind his popularity and success as a leader.

All leaders have enemies who try to pull them down, more so when their popularity is on the rise. Krishna was no different. His uncle, cousins and other relatives were jealous of his power, which was his popularity, and tried to destroy him. But then, as it happens with great leaders, Krishna continued to lead people on the right path. With the help of his followers, he destroyed his enemies. He helped people to accomplish their goals and in the process, accomplished his own—the well-being of his people and his country.

Tish Baldrige, an American etiquette expert famous as having been Jacqueline Kennedy's social secretary, has summarized it well, 'Good manners are cost effective. They not only increase the quality of life in the workplace, they contribute to employee morale, embellish the company image, and play a major role in generating profit.'

Seems quite a handful! Yet, there is more that we can achieve by following the right work etiquette:

1. Building trust
2. Promoting positivity
3. Reflecting confidence
4. Preventing misunderstanding

Building trust: Our behaviour helps us build relationships in life. In a workplace, observing the right work etiquette entails a similar response. We tend to bond better with the management as well as our colleagues, clients and vendors. People appreciate honesty in business dealings, which results in creating trust in the clients. Consistent professionalism and integrity in our behaviour also generates loyalty in the people with whom we are dealing. Proper work etiquette is the backbone of a successful organization.

Promoting positivity: Good work etiquette fosters a positive work environment. When the management and the employees treat each other with respect and sensitivity, the organization most certainly grows and prospers. When the team leader makes his subordinates feel comfortable, the productivity of his team increases manyfold. A seed always grows into a healthy plant when it is nurtured well. An effective leader is like a competent gardener, he creates a positive nurturing environment for his team, which naturally gives positive results.

Reflecting confidence: Observing work etiquette is reflective of our own persona. It shows our strong moral and ethical foundation, makes us worthy of trust, and instils confidence in our colleagues and subordinates. A confident approach helps the organization to grow. Customers and vendors feel secure working with such an organization. Self-confidence is an immense morale booster—it makes a person feel that he can handle all kinds of situations and accomplish much more. Work efficiency automatically grows, as does the output.

Preventing misunderstanding: Misunderstandings happen in an organization because of miscommunication. If work etiquette were adhered to, everyone would be treating everyone else professionally. They would be toeing the lines and communication would be clear. There would be no grey areas, and even if they did appear, they would be resolved quickly. This kind of smooth working would help in the growth of the organization as well as the people working in it.

Good work etiquette is the mantra for advancing on the career path. Having good communication skills and the ability to listen go a long way in impressing our seniors in the business.

Netiquette, or etiquette in online communication, is also a crucial part of work etiquette. Since virtual communication is essential to businesses now, it is important to maintain professionalism on emails as well.

Business breakfasts and luncheons are getting very popular; hence tableside etiquette has also become a part of work etiquette.

There are eight golden work etiquette tips that make our lives smoother at any workplace:

1. Recognize everyone's role
2. Make every meeting useful
3. Communicate promptly
4. Respect others' time
5. Dress for the part
6. Respect other cultures
7. Stick to timelines
8. Remember the basic manners

Recognize everyone's role: We should remember at all times that any work in an organization is teamwork. All members of the team have a role to play in the larger picture. We need to value that role. When we value each member, we encourage him or her to work harder, do better and grow. With the growth of each member, the organization also grows.

Make every meeting useful: Meetings are meant to discuss issues, to resolve problems and to plan strategies for the future. Most meetings should be successful, but some may just end up as a waste of time. Yet, we can still get some useful insight out of them. The most important thing is to table all the meetings and send the minutes to every attendee of the meeting, along with our comments. This documentation would be useful in understanding the loopholes and failures.

Communicate promptly: Every communication, whether verbal, telephonic, or via email or text messages, should be responded to on time. Timely response indicates that we respect the other person's time. This generates respect for us too.

Respect others' time: In any workplace, everyone is busy and if we need anyone's help, we need to ask politely for their time. Once given, we should not misuse it; we should take whatever help that we need and get on with our work as soon as possible. And as a rule, meetings should not be interrupted unless there is an emergency.

Dress for the part: Most organizations normally have a flexible dress code. It is very important to dress for the part, as they say. Clothes that attract instant attention are not appreciated. The work clothes should be functional yet dignified, keeping in mind that we are the face of our organization at all times.

Respect other cultures: The world is shrinking. Everyone is working everywhere. We get to see multicultural set-ups in most organizations now. It is important to make each member of the organization comfortable by celebrating different cultural festivals in the workplace. When people travel far away from their home country to come and work in our country, it becomes our duty to make them feel welcome.

Stick to timelines: All work is time-related. And it is important to stick to timelines and deadlines. All work is interconnected too. If we deliver late, the client suffers, and finally the end-user suffers. It causes a ripple effect and eventually translates into losses for our company. The solution is that we tweak our own timelines, so that we deliver before time.

Remember the basic manners: The basic manners of saying 'please', 'thank you', 'sorry', 'excuse me', not using offensive language, not speaking in a loud voice, etc. hold true everywhere—at home, at school and even at our workplace.

Observing work etiquette is something that we can consciously cultivate and then it becomes a habit. Once that happens, we will get to know, as we will see the circle of people we get along with growing steadily. Our path to success will become clearer then.

Remember, real success is not about getting millions of virtual followers on social media. It's about getting along with real people, if Krishna's success is anything to go by.

18.

Krishna on Time Management

Either run the day or the day runs you.

Time management can be simply explained as the ability to use time effectively and productively.

This is a very vital part of our lives. Right from childhood, our days were spread out over timetables and calendars. Our parents or caregivers planned our waking hours. In school, the timetables were fixed and they were made according to the syllabi we had to complete by the end of the year, which in turn was allocated according to the certificate we were aiming for, like high school, etc. So we find that knowingly or unknowingly, our time has been managed from practically the time we were born. Yes, our food was too!

Once we are old enough to handle our lives ourselves, we start managing our time according to our needs and goals. The same basic principle is applied in work as well. We need to figure out our short-term and long-term goals and plan our time at our workplace accordingly.

If we don't, then we run into problems in the following three areas:

1. Workflow

2. Deadlines
3. Quality of work

Workflow: If we haven't prioritized our short-term goals, we are likely to waste a lot of time jumping from one to the other. Our efficiency would drop. Our productivity would also drop. Overall, a lot of time and energy would be wasted without showing any substantial result.

Deadlines: Every task has a deadline. If our workflow is inefficient due to lack of proper prioritisation, it would slow down our productivity. In such a scenario, it is evident that the deadlines would be difficult to meet.

Quality of work: Inefficient workflow results in last-minute rush to meet the deadlines. Invariably, the quality is compromised for speed. Ideally, time is set aside for quality check, but where time is not managed properly, the quality tends to get ignored.

It may happen that we get to know of our time management—or I should say mismanagement—issues only after we have lost a deal. The prudent thing to do would be to note the signs and symptoms of the malady before it takes a serious turn and causes permanent damage.

Red flags of time mismanagement:

1. Being habitually late
2. In a constant rush
3. Getting impatient
4. Poor performance
5. Lack of energy

Being habitually late: When we are not motivated by the goal, we tend to become casual. Or we take on too much on our plate without realizing that we can do only so much. Multitasking is not everyone's cup of tea. These are some of the common reasons behind people being habitually late. Once the motivation is there and the goal becomes our priority, we should be able to manage our time better. And with our time management in place, being late would be unthinkable.

In a constant rush: Clearly, if we are unable to manage our time properly, we would always be missing something here and would be rushing for something else there. The entire thing becomes a vicious cycle. A better time management would ensure that all things get done on time.

Getting impatient: If we are unable to manage our time properly and start missing deadlines, we are bound to get impatient. Prioritising tasks will help in saving on time and maintaining patience.

Poor performance: Our performance at work takes a hit the moment we are under stress. Rushing to meet deadlines is one such stress. The genesis is mismanagement of time. If tasks are slotted on a timetable, the deadlines would be taken care of. And a major stress is over when deadlines are met comfortably, resulting in our maintaining optimal performance.

Lack of energy: It's all in our mind, as they say. If we are unable to meet deadlines, or if our performance is dipping, our stresses would increase. Missing appointments and rushing to meet deadlines are all due to gross mismanagement of time. Once that starts happening, we are in a state of permanent chaos in the workplace, which naturally results in chaotic thoughts. All that activity in the brain makes us feel mentally exhausted. And because the brain is tired already, any work we do seems like a heavy chore. Better time management results in better brain-body coordination and higher energy levels.

If we spot any of the red flags mentioned above, we should stop and rework our timetable.

'It's not enough to be busy; so are the ants. The question is, what are we busy about?' said Henry David Thoreau, a key proponent of transcendentalism.

Being busy does not mean we are managing our time well. Getting more work done also does not mean we are managing our time well. Focusing on getting the important tasks done well is the key to effective time management. Priorities make all the difference.

St. Francis of Assisi gave an interesting time management tip: 'Start by doing what's necessary; then do what's possible; and suddenly you are doing the impossible.'

Let's see where and how Krishna used his time management skills.

In the battle of Mahabharata, when Arjun came to know that senior Kaurava warriors killed his son Abhimanyu callously while the latter was unarmed and injured, he decided to take revenge. He was told that it was the Sindhu king Jayadrath who effectively stopped the Pandavas from entering the discus formation of Kaurava warriors behind Abhimanyu, as was planned by them, thus trapping the young boy.

Arjun swore that he would kill Jayadrath the next day, positively before sunset, or else burn himself to death. In those times, war would be like a nine-to-five job. It would end by sunset and the warriors would relax and prepare for the next day.

Since this declaration of Arjun reached the Kaurava forces, they decided to protect Jayadrath till sunset. The plan was that Arjun, like the true warrior that he was, would certainly fulfil his oath and being unable to kill Jayadrath, he would set fire to himself. With Arjun dead, the Kauravas would easily win the war.

This seemed quite easy and the Kauravas did manage to stall Arjun for the entire day. The moment he would get close to Jayadrath, someone would intervene and then Arjun would have to fight with him. Towards the close of the day, the Kauravas had managed to create a fair bit of distance between Jayadrath and Arjun. It was a matter of hours now and the sun would set. But inflamed with the thought of his son's slaughter, Arjun fought with fury. Brandishing weapons in both his hands, he ploughed on through the Kaurava forces like living death.

Everyone looked towards the west, some wanting the sun to set, others not wanting so. Suddenly, there was darkness and there were cries of joy in the Kaurava forces.

Jayadrath looked towards the west and could not see the sun. He was jubilant, thinking he was safe now and that Arjun would immolate himself soon.

At that moment, Krishna said to Arjun, 'Jayadrath is looking at the horizon. He doesn't know that I have caused this darkness. The sun has not set as yet. Do your job, now that Jayadrath is off his guard.'

Arjun took his aim and shot an arrow that sliced off Jayadrath's head from his body. The sun shone again. And Jayadrath was dead, as per Arjun's oath.

Krishna had to do this tweaking of time to run the day; otherwise the day would have run them.

This happens all the time in any organization, and in life too. If we do not manage time, time starts managing us. Time management is life management.

Time management not only reduces stress and anxiety, it also frees up time to pursue more opportunities. Those who manage their time well are able to achieve their goals better and do so in a shorter period of time.

There are five ways to manage time effectively:

1. Setting the right goals
2. Prioritising the tasks
3. Making timelines
4. Taking breaks
5. Planning ahead

Setting the right goals: Setting specific, measurable and attainable goals is the first logical step to managing time effectively. If the goal is vast, it becomes vague. After all, the target has to be limited enough to focus on.

Prioritising the tasks: A goal is reached by working through a number of tasks. We need to make a list of all the possible tasks related to our goal. Then we need to make a gross list separating the essential from the non-essential, like grain from chaff. Our attention should be on prioritising the essential tasks.

Making timelines: This is the most important step in time management. Once the tasks are prioritized, they should be placed on a calendar. Each task should be mapped on a timeline with a deadline. It's quite like making a timetable to study for an exam. We need to complete the studies, do the practice, revise—all within a limited time frame.

Taking breaks: Non-stop work ultimately results in physical and mental fatigue, which eventually affects our productivity as well as the quality of our work. It is important to take short breaks in between tasks so that our energy levels get time to recover. This increases efficiency in work and also mental clarity to tackle any untoward issues.

Planning ahead: We should always plan in advance. It helps in streamlining our actions. Once our timelines and deadlines are in place, we would be saving on time. Planning in advance would also facilitate taking breaks, which in turn would keep our mind fresh. This further gives us mental space to plan for our next goal.

This was time management at a macro level. But time also has to be effectively managed at a micro level.

There are 12 basic steps to conscious time management:

1. Assessing time spent
2. Determining desired results
3. Creating deadlines
4. Using the weekend to plan the week
5. Making a daily plan
6. Making a 'done' list
7. Blocking out distractions

8. Avoiding multitasking
9. Avoiding clutter
10. Training the other side of the brain
11. Looking after our health
12. Learning to say 'No'

Assessing time spent: It is important to start by inspecting and assessing the time we spend on various tasks. This would help us in identifying unproductive tasks vis-a-vis the time spent on them. These tasks should be removed or replaced from the plan.

Determining desired results: If the agenda of any meeting is well defined then its desired result are also known. Keeping that in mind, any meeting that does not yield the desired result should be reconvened with a modified agenda, instead of wasting time to figure out why the outcome was not what we had wanted.

Creating deadlines: This is a very important step in macro as well as micro time management. Setting time constraints to any task makes us pay more attention to it. With improved focus, efficiency also improves. In case we find ourselves crossing the deadline, we can immediately revisit the task to see where we could have wasted time—for instance taking unscheduled breaks, etc.—and reset the schedule.

Using the weekend to plan the week: Weekends are certainly for relaxing, but we can surely take out a few minutes and quickly revise the plan for the coming week. This should be done to check that everything is in order; the resources are in place; and in case the week gone by has some leftover tasks, they are incorporated in the schedule for the coming week. This way, we can start our working week with a well-sorted head.

Making a daily plan: Apart from task allocation for the day, micro planning of the day is also important. All days are not the same and we also don't function with the same energy level every day. So, first thing before starting the day should be planning the day. That way we will utilize our time and energy optimally to give the best results.

Making a 'done' list: This exercise is to boost our morale and encourage us to keep going. Every completed task should be noted on the 'done' list on a daily basis. We cannot expect to be congratulated on the completion of each and every task, but we can surely congratulate ourselves over the weekend when we see our 'done' list. This helps us boost our self-confidence for the coming week, reflecting in the increase of our efficiency and productivity.

Blocking out distractions: Distractions slow us down and result in wastage of time. The best way to avoid distractions in work is to allocate 'break time' to them. Self-discipline, in terms of which phone calls to take during work and which to ignore, helps in keeping distractions at bay. Online distractions can be avoided by going offline while working, depending on the nature of work, of course.

Avoiding multitasking: Multitasking is overrated. It actually is unable to do full justice to all the tasks being handled. Somewhere or the other we would fall short. Prioritising still remains the best option, where at least each task gets our complete attention.

Avoiding clutter: A cluttered workstation, cluttered room, or even a cluttered computer, all indicate chaos and confusion. And that is reflected in us. For our brains to work systematically, we need to introduce the proper systems in our environment. We need to keep our workplaces clean and tidy and our living spaces neat and clean. Our computers should also have the various files and folders in some order, either alphabetically or priority-wise.

Training the other side of the brain: It's a proven fact that periodically getting out of our comfort zone leads us to success. It trains that part of our brain which we do not use much in our work. So, hobbies like dancing and singing would help a lawyer, and martial arts would help a painter, to enhance their creativity and problem-solving capabilities.

Looking after our health: This is one thing that tends to get neglected till it's too late. And then it impacts our work; our efficiency and productivity get compromised; our quality of work drops and we lose deadlines and clients. 'Prevention is better than cure' is a wise saying. And that is exactly what we have to factor for in our timetables. We have to make time for exercise, at least thrice a week if not more. We also need to slot in some 'me time' to relax completely. Just as we look after our computers and cars, getting them serviced regularly so that they serve us well, so we have to look after our own body for it to function the way we want it to and for as long as we want it to.

Learning to say 'No': This might be the toughest thing to do for some, but is very important for effective time management. We have to keep in mind that our time is precious and has to be managed effectively. We cannot afford to spend it on things that do not align with our mission or goal.

Micromanagement of time helps us to run the day, leading to effective time management for a larger purpose. We cannot allow the day to run us, can we now?

19.

Krishna on Greed

Greed fails even the greedy in the end.

Greed is an intense, selfish and insatiable desire for material gain or power. A wise man once said, 'Greed is a bottomless pit that exhausts the person in an endless effort to satisfy the need without ever reaching satisfaction.'

A closer look into greed shows that its not always about material gain. It is about the security and independence that wealth can bring to a person. Wealth itself is not bad, but a greedy person develops too much attachment to it and has excessive desire for it. And this excess takes him down the wrong path.

And not only for wealth; desire or need could be for anything. And consumption of anything without moderation becomes a destructive force, which is constantly propelled by greed.

We are familiar with how greed for food impacts our health and gives rise to most of the diseases. Good taste coupled with the feeling of happiness makes people eat more than what their body needs, till it turns into a craving. It's the greed of continuing the feeling of mental relaxation that pushes people towards alcoholism and addiction to drugs.

Greed pushes a person or even a country to lose their sense of balance. To take an example: a small country decides to devote itself to growing cash crops to meet the needs of larger countries. The smaller country forsakes its diversity of crops in order to earn money to look after its infrastructure needs. Though this would be a need-based greed, but the ultimate result would be an ecological disaster.

Obsessed with acquisitions, people take huge risks at the cost of their own mental peace, which finally affects their health and relationships. In any case, greedy people are never able to sustain good personal or professional relationships, as they are constantly planning their next moves and are not really engaging with the person at hand. Greed, as they say, is not a financial issue, but an issue of the heart. When greed lives in our heart, there is no place left for anyone or anything else.

Greed blinds people. They feel that if all has gone well till now, it's not likely to change anytime soon. Also, when they see others behaving the same way, they feel validated.

Deforestation is another malady that has stemmed from greed. People seem to have forgotten or are ignoring the history of civilizations across the globe. Inter-clan competition driven by greed made the people start destroying nature in order to hoard resources, till eventually nature destroyed them. Animals and plants became extinct, and so did many tribes of humans who had no resources left to sustain them with.

Pulitzer Prize winner Thomas Friedman writes in his book, *Hot, Flat and Crowded*, 'The way we were creating wealth had built up so many toxic assets in both the financial world and the natural world that by 2008/9, it shook the very foundation of our markets and ecosystems. That's right, while they might not appear on the surface to have been related, the destabilisation of both the Market and Mother Nature had the same root causes... The same recklessness undermined them.'

It is true that greed is the reason why people irrationally over-invest and plunder our natural resources. They desire to get as much as possible for themselves without thinking of the consequences for future generations. They feel they have the right to improve the quality of their own lives and they certainly can afford to do so, except that they do it at a huge cost to humanity.

Mahatma Gandhi said, 'There is enough in the world for man's need but not for man's greed.'

There are four signs to identify greed:

1. Lack of satisfaction
2. Envy
3. Lack of empathy
4. Self-centred behaviour

Lack of satisfaction: This is the first obvious character of a greedy person. They are never satisfied with what they have. They always want more and then more. And that 'more' is unending.

Envy: This is one step ahead of greed. It is like greed plus one—not only do these people want more of what they already have, but they also want what others have.

Lack of empathy: This is quite understandable, since a greedy person is so consumed by his own greed that he cannot see beyond it. These people have no interest in the feelings of others and hence, it doesn't matter to them even if others are hurt by their actions.

Self-centred behaviour: This is the hallmark of a greedy person. Everything is about them and for them. It's 'I, me, mine' all through for them. They know no limits in pursuing their greed. In an organization, they would manipulate their colleagues and take credit for as many tasks as possible. A greedy team leader would be more interested in grabbing his bonus rather than sharing it with the team. Greedy people do not think twice before compromising their moral or ethical values; they are always looking out for loopholes to outsmart rules or laws to get what they want.

All the above signs were present in Duryodhan, the eldest of the Kaurava brothers. He was full of envy for his cousins, the Pandavas, and wished them nothing but the worst. His greed for power made him suppress the Pandavas. He was very destructive, and made the destruction of the Pandavas his life's mission.

Duryodhan's greed started right from his childhood days. The Pandava brothers came to Hastinapur after their father's death and started living with their cousins the Kauravas. That's when they first met and their rivalry began.

Pandu was originally the king of Hastinapur, but because of a sin he committed, he decided to abdicate the throne and live in the forest like a hermit, to do penance. His two wives were with him and they had five sons in the forest, called the Pandavas.

Pandu's blind brother Dhritarashtra became the king of Hastinapur by default. He had a hundred and one sons called the Kauravas, and a daughter.

As the cousins grew up, studied and trained together, sibling rivalry started setting in. Duryodhan, the eldest of the Kaurava children, felt that the presence of the Pandava brothers in their palace was a threat to his inheritance of the throne.

His logic was simple. Yudhishthir was the eldest son of Pandu, who had been king of Hastinapur before Duryodhan's own father Dhritarashtra was given the throne. So, it was very likely that Yudhishthir would want to be the king after Dhritarashtra.

The catch was that Dhritarashtra was older than Pandu, but because he was blind and considered unfit, Pandu had been made the king. Since his father was the older of the two brothers, Duryodhan felt that as Dhritarashtra's son, he was lawfully the heir to the throne of Hastinapur.

This greed for the throne became Duryodhan's driving force throughout his life.

He hated the Pandavas anyway, but in particular, Duryodhan hated the second Pandava Bheem the most. Bheem had a large built and was physically very powerful. And he loved playing pranks and bullying his cousins. Out of sheer malice, one day, Duryodhan tried to kill Bheem by feeding him poison-laced sweets. Bheem survived that, and the Pandavas realized that Duryodhan's hatred towards them was very real.

While the princes were training for warfare, Duryodhan saw how great an archer Arjun was. Bheem was good at wrestling and fighting with a mace. Duryodhan could match Bheem, but not Arjun. As luck would have it, Karna challenged Arjun at archery in front of everyone when the princes were showcasing their warfare skills in front of the entire kingdom. Duryodhan grabbed the opportunity and declared Karna, who had been a commoner till then, as the king of the kingdom of Anga. This one deed bought Karna's loyalty towards Duryodhan for life. Karna became Duryodhan's asset as a great archer. Now, he felt, with Karna by his side, he would be able to defeat the Pandavas in any battle, if it ever came to that.

Following Duryodhan's life shows how greed can make a person so malignant and conniving.

His second attempt to kill the Pandavas was worse than the first. Duryodhan and his cronies convinced King Dhritarashtra to send the Pandavas along with their mother to a nearby temple town for a visit. Meanwhile, an extremely inflammable house was built with wax, lac and other combustible items, to house the Pandava family. The plan was to set the house on fire once the Pandavas had comfortably settled in. The town was far away from Hastinapur, so the blame of arson could not possibly be traced back to Duryodhan. It seemed like a clever plan, but it didn't work either. The spy network was strong even in those days; the Pandavas got to know of the plan and escaped.

Seeing the burnt ruins of their house, people assumed the Pandava family to be dead. Knowing well that if news got out of their being still alive, Duryodhan was capable of sending his goons to kill them, the Pandavas decided to go underground for a while.

Once the Pandavas got married to princess Draupadi of Panchal, the news had to reach Hastinapur. The elders of the family promptly invited the Pandavas, along with their mother and wife, back to Hastinapur. This time, King Dhritarashtra gave a piece of a wasteland to the Pandava family to live on.

The hardworking Pandavas converted that wasteland into a fantastic township called Indraprastha. The eldest Pandava Yudhishthir became its ruler. And suddenly the Pandavas were back in the limelight. People praised them, their rule and their township to the skies. And Duryodhan was struck with envy.

This time, hatred, envy and greed got together and Duryodhan started plotting to usurp Indraprastha. He invited Yudhishthir to play dice with him, and in that fraudulent game, made him lose Indraprastha. Not only that, the Pandavas, along with their wife, were also sentenced to a 13 year exile. Duryodhan was hell-bent on destroying the Pandavas.

After completing the tenure of their exile, when the Pandavas staked a claim on their property, Duryodhan refused to relent. He would rather fight to kill than give an inch of land to his cousins. This led to the great battle of Mahabharata.

As the preparations for the imminent war started, Duryodhan and Arjun approached Krishna for his support. Krishna gave two options: his armed forces or he himself unarmed. Arjun took the latter while Duryodhan was very happy to get Krishna's army to join his forces in the war. He felt that an unarmed Krishna would be quite useless. At that moment, too, Duryodhan was only interested in increasing his forces to rout the Pandavas in the impending war.

Before the actual battle commenced, Krishna tried to talk Duryodhan out of it. He explained that it was just his greed that was making him take such a foolhardy decision. A compromise was possible, as the Pandavas were open to be given just five small villages instead of their much larger and grander Indraprastha.

Duryodhan's parents had also realized by now that their son was not the right fit for the kingship of Hastinapur, but old as they were, they were helpless. Driven by intense greed, their eldest son had become unstoppable.

The battle of Mahabharata resulted in victory for the Pandavas. The entire Kaurava clan was killed. In the end, Duryodhan died alone, unsung. His own greed had failed him.

Greed is probably the biggest sickness plaguing the world today. It harms the greedy and also those around them. From climate change to civil wars to dictatorial leaders of some countries, greed is the root cause of all the evils of today.

Overcoming greed is a huge task, but not impossible. There are seven ways that can help us combat and overcome greed:

1. Developing compassion for others
2. Sharing with others
3. Remembering those who have helped us
4. Remembering those who didn't help us when they could
5. Doing our bit for the world
6. Being content
7. Recognizing impermanence

Developing compassion for others: We should meet people who are hurting or are in dire need; it would make us see the other side of the world. The real world is not just within the bubble that we live in; it is out there. Once we feel compassion for those who are going through hardships, our greed will melt away.

Sharing with others: Giving is a good habit to cultivate. Sharing from what we have in abundance cannot make us any poorer.

Remembering those who have helped us: We should take out some time to consciously remember those people who have helped us reach where we are today. The list would be long. This exercise would teach us humility; it would tell us that without help nobody reaches anywhere.

Remembering those who didn't help us when they could: This is not to take revenge, but to take care that we don't do the same to others.

Doing our bit for the world: If we want the world to be a better place, we should try to contribute in making it so. We should help those organizations that are involved in helping the helpless.

Being content: This is the most important feeling, which most people miss out on. If we can learn to be content with what we have, we would forget the lust for more. This is in the context of wealth. In a work scenario, the greed for reaching higher levels in our profession, or expanding our business operations should not be driven by money but by personal growth. We need to remember that money would come automatically with personal growth.

Recognizing impermanence: Nothing lives forever. Wealth also comes and goes. Time changes and it may happen that the ones whom we rejected as useless may become useful to us, so we should be kind to everyone.

Greed is blinding. It takes away people from reality. They forget that they would die one day and then all the wealth that they have amassed will be left behind. If we transfer our love for money to a love for life, we will not be bothered by greed.

Since, according to Krishna, greed fails even the greedy in the end, isn't it rather silly to engage with it on our way to success!

20.

Krishna on Loyalty

Loyalty goes both ways; if you don't return it, you don't deserve it.

Loyalty is allegiance. It is a bond of faithfulness. Unfortunately, it gets taken for granted till we experience disloyalty or betrayal.

In an organization, an employee's loyalty is based on the employer's loyalty. When the employees come to know that if they efficiently do the job that they were hired for, the employer will support them, their loyalty for their employer strengthens.

But then, such loyalty runs the risk of being converted into 'blind loyalty', which is dangerous. Why? People who are blindly loyal in their relationships tend to forgive the indiscretions or betrayals of their partners or friends and eventually this erodes their self-esteem. An employee who is blindly loyal to his employer does the same thing; in fact it's worse, because the employer might be asking him to do illegal activities.

Absolute loyalty, which, like blind loyalty, follows a person or organization, including whatever they stand for, their beliefs, practices and expected behaviour, is like slavery.

Our loyalty should be to our own values and principles first.

Though loyalty is a positive trait, we get to see negative consequences of it as well. Loyalty to a cause may result in fanatical violence; loyalty to family may result in nepotism; and loyalty to political leaders overlooks their crimes and turns them into heroes.

The worst is loyalty for money, which is actually greed in the garb of loyalty. These days we see players of every sport switching their allegiance to clubs and organizations that pay better. And professionals keep changing their companies for better remuneration packages. The earlier focus of loyalty to a job or task at hand has now shifted to what goes into the pocket.

All that we have discussed above are cases of misplaced loyalty. When we are loyal to people or organizations that we shouldn't be loyal to; when we are so biased towards a person or an organization that we defend them for the wrong reasons, then our loyalty is most definitely misplaced.

Misplaced loyalty could be because of some force or threat being used by the said person or organization, or it could even be a simple case of emotional attachment or guilt. Whatever the reasons for it, misplaced loyalty is always taken for granted and abused. And eventually, it results in varied consequences from dissatisfaction to frustration to even depression.

Why? Because at the end of the day, our heart knows that what we are doing is wrong. Unfortunately, by that time we are stuck. In order to avoid such a situation, we have to inculcate in us a healthy understanding of right and wrong, and act responsibly.

Loyalty is like a double-edged sword. We need to understand how to use it right. And as they say, respect is earned, honesty is appreciated, trust is gained, and loyalty is returned. It is reciprocative.

Krishna had a childhood friend, a classmate from school, called Sudama. They were very good friends. As it happens with all of us, they grew up and went their separate ways.

Sudama was from a poor brahmin family, who earned their living by teaching and conducting various religious rituals for people of their village. Krishna belonged to the rich and powerful family of the Yadavas in Dwarka. The class difference between the two was pretty wide.

Many years passed and there was no contact between the two friends, as is understandable, keeping in view Krishna's hectic schedule of life. Meanwhile, Sudama had married and continued to live an impoverished life, trying to make ends meet with great difficulty. He had told his wife about Krishna, the good times they had as children, and how much they loved each other. Initially, she heard the story and felt happy for her husband; later on, it started bothering her. What was the point of having a wealthy friend like Krishna, if they were not being benefitted by his wealth?

Poor Sudama was a very shy person. He could not even dream of asking anyone for help, let alone a big and important man like Krishna. He kept on ignoring his wife's nagging, till finally, it became too much for even a patient man like him. He agreed to visit Krishna.

Since it was customary in those times to take a gift when visiting someone, Sudama's wife gave him a little packet of rice flakes for Krishna. That was all they had at home as food.

Sudama walked all the way to Dwarka. On reaching Krishna's palatial house, he hesitated at the huge gates. Suddenly he lost his nerve and regretted listening to his wife. He was about to turn back, when the guards asked him his name and the reason for his visit.

Sudama did not dare to mention the reason for his visit, nor could he say that he was an old friend of Krishna. He could barely mumble out his name. Seeing his dust-filled, tattered clothes and his tired face, the guards gave him some water to drink and made him wait in the shade, while one of them went inside to inform Krishna.

Krishna was having a meal with his wife Rukmini when the guard announced Sudama's name. He instantly dropped everything, got up and rushed outside to receive his beloved old friend, to the shock of all who watched. Sudama was overwhelmed with emotion, seeing that Krishna still recognized him. He could barely talk.

Krishna hugged Sudama warmly and took him inside, holding his hand affectionately. Rukmini was also pleased to meet her husband's old friend. She organized for Sudama to bathe and dress in new clothes. Once freshened up, the two friends ate a sumptuous meal together, talking of old times. Krishna wanted to know every little detail of Sudama's life after they left school, so there was a lot to talk about.

At night, Sudama was given a comfortable bed to sleep in. The next morning, after breakfast, Sudama said to his dear friend that he wanted to take his leave. Krishna said, 'But you still haven't told me why you came to meet me.' Sudama was too embarrassed to say anything. He just mumbled something about not having met for so long, etc.

Krishna told his attendants to get Sudama ready for his journey. Sudama's old clothes were washed and given back to him. He wore them and was ready to say his goodbyes. Rukmini was shocked to see all this.

As Sudama was leaving, Krishna stopped him again. This time he said, 'Why haven't you given me the gift that you have brought for me?' Sudama was taken aback at this query. He looked around for his little packet of rice flakes. When Krishna finally found it, he tore it open, exclaiming, 'I knew you must have brought the good old snack from our childhood days for me, just like you did in school!'

With the acutely embarrassed Sudama watching, Krishna started eating the rice flakes, gobbling them in mouthfuls. Then he saw Sudama off at the gates, cheerfully telling his friend to convey his regards to his wife and thank her for the rice flakes.

When Krishna came in after seeing off Sudama, Rukmini asked him why he took back his friend's new clothes. Why did he allow him to return in his tattered old clothes and that too, empty-handed? Krishna responded, 'I don't want people to think my friend came to meet me with a hidden agenda. I want them to see that my old friend still loved me as before and was still as loyal to me as before. Our changing status in life has not affected our relationship.'

Meanwhile, Sudama had left Krishna's house feeling exhilarated. The poor, simple man was happy that his old childhood friend actually remembered him, had recognized him after so many years, and had treated him the same way as he did in their school days. He knew that he was returning home empty-handed, but his heart was so full of love and gratitude for Krishna, that he didn't care about what his wife might say on his return.

On reaching his village, Sudama couldn't see his old hut. It was gone and in its place stood a beautiful, big house. Sudama stood at the main gate, wondering where to look for his wife, when he saw her coming out, laughing and crying in happiness. She was dressed in fine clothes and jewels. What was happening?

Sudama's wife told him that it was all Krishna's doing. He repaid his old friend's loyalty by sharing his wealth with him, and that too without asking. It was a wonderful case of loyalty being reciprocated.

Good leaders inspire loyalty is an oft-repeated management cliché, but whatever the sceptics might feel, it does hold true. If people believe they share values with their leader or their organization, they stay loyal to them. They reciprocate.

That happens at the macro level. At the micro level, the relationship between an employer and employee has changed over the years, especially in terms of loyalty and commitment.

An employee owes his organization a good day's work, and his best effort, however boring the task may be. It sounds normal and expected, but these days there is rider attached to it: The same employee would expect a raise in six months and may leave for a better opportunity in a year.

According to the Forbes Human Resources Council survey of 2017, millennials are three times more likely than the older generation to change their jobs.

Why? Well, loyalty to an organization requires the employee to refrain from any action that is contrary to the organization's interest. But sticking to the same job forever and not leaving for better prospects are not part of this. Millennials stick to the word of law.

This leaves the responsibility of generating the old-fashioned loyalty in the employees to the leadership of the organization. Management guru Patrick Lencioni couldn't be more right in saying, 'When leaders throughout an organization take an active, genuine interest in the people they manage, when they invest real time to understand employees at a fundamental level, they create a climate for greater morale, loyalty, and yes, growth.'

Leaders who possess strong work ethics embody four principles that guide their work behaviour and inspire loyalty in their subordinates:

1. Being reliable
2. Being dedicated
3. Being productive
4. Being cooperative

Being reliable: Reliability and dependability go hand in hand. If we say we will be present for a meeting, we not only need to be present but be on time as well. A fleeting presence won't do. Punctuality plays a big role in reliability. And reliability results in consistency of performance.

Being dedicated: Commitment to the post we are handling makes us put extra hours in our work at times. Our dedication filters down and encourages our subordinates to become more involved as well. The more involved one gets in their work, the less likely it is that they will leave in a hurry.

Being productive: Leaders who don't quit till the task is successfully completed are role models for their teams. Dedication and consistency in performance makes a person more productive.

Being cooperative: This is an important asset to have when one is working in an organization. It is all about teamwork. To have a good team, the leader himself should be a good team player. After all, it's the captain of the team who generates loyalty of the team towards their mission.

Once we have an effective leader with strong work ethics in place, the next step to generate loyalty in the workforce would be to establish a work environment reflecting the leadership.

There are three basic steps to achieve that:

1. Establishing behavioural policies
2. Appointing an ombudsman
3. Encouraging teamwork

Establishing behavioural policies: It is very important for an organization, whatever the size, to have a list of acceptable and unacceptable behaviours. Apart from that, the levels of punishment for unacceptable behaviour should be spelt out in detail. This exercise is imperative to make the team members feel comfortable and secure in their workplace. It also acts as a deterrent to the mischievous elements of the company. When the workplace feels as secure as home, the loyalty levels of the people working there shoot up. They are assured that the organization is concerned with their welfare.

Appointing an ombudsman: Setting up a helpline is a crucial step in the direction of making the employees feel that they have a voice. Having an ombudsman to investigate serious issues goes a long way in generating employee trust. Once they sense the freedom of voicing their opinions, even against the management, they would work better. It is important for an employee to feel that he matters to the organization. This is reciprocated by his loyalty.

Encouraging teamwork: Encouraging teamwork helps the team members to bond with each other. They make friends and share their problems. Simply talking to a colleague may solve many trivial problems. It is like a family, where minor issues are resolved over meals. This kind of bonding also generates loyalty to colleagues and eventually the organization.

Loyalty is about staying true to a person or an organization, even behind their backs. Sudama was true to Krishna even behind his back. He was also true to his work of spreading education in society. And that was why he remained poor; he could have switched to another more lucrative line of work. He didn't, because he was loyal to his duty as a teacher. Krishna saw all that and reciprocated by rewarding Sudama with whatever he needed.

Krishna did not want to show to the world that Sudama entered his house in tatters and came out in riches. That would have given the wrong impression: that Sudama had come to ask for money. Krishna respected his friend and his loyalty, and wanted the world to see that.

Reciprocation of Sudama's loyalty, and that of many more before and after him, made Krishna a true leader, deserving of all the loyalty he received in his lifetime. That loyalty still continues.

No wonder, then, that Krishna is considered the finest management guru that mankind has ever come across!

Acknowledgments

There have been many people in my life, some no more and some still around, who have taught me, mostly unknowingly, whatever I needed to learn to reach where I am today. I will always be grateful to them.

I am grateful to Kapish Mehra for giving me this opportunity to express myself. Seeing his passion for books and understanding of the audience, I have no reservation in saying that I would like our association to continue for as long as it can.

I feel blessed to be surrounded by my family, my support system, giving me space to continue writing.

I am forever grateful to my readers and my publishers, who are my extended family, without whose continuous appreciation and encouragement, I wouldn't have been labelled as an 'author' today.

Lastly, I would like to acknowledge my reference books: *Mahabharata Retold* by C. Rajagopalachari, *Srimad Bhagavatam* translated by Anand Aadhar and Bankim Chandra Chattopadhyaya's *Krishna Charitra*.